UP & RUNNING

Gray ~ SHACK

CHOCS

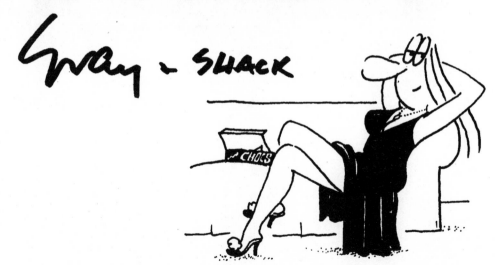

This book is dedicated to

(Your name)...

With thanks for the money

UP & RUNNING

THE ADVENTURES OF CHLOË & CO

by Gray & SHACK

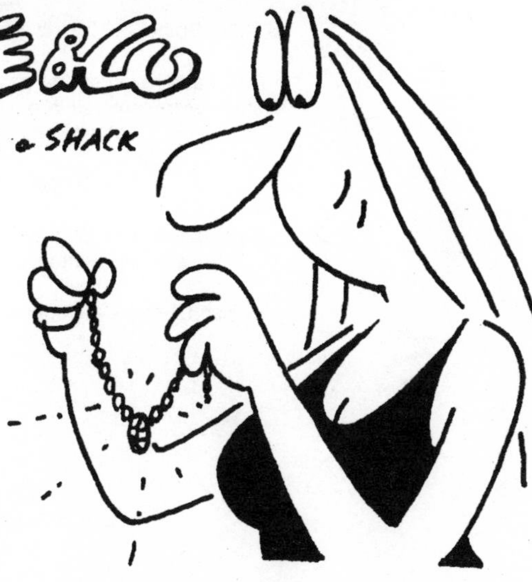

metro

First published in Great Britain in 1998
by Metro Books (an imprint of Metro Publishing Limited), 19 Gerrard Street, London W1V 7LA

British Library Cataloguing in Publication Data. A CIP record of this book is available on
request from the British Library.

ISBN 1 900512 50 5

10 9 8 7 6 5 4 3 2 1

Typeset and designed by Don Macpherson
Printed in Great Britain by Redwood Books, Trowbridge, Wiltshire

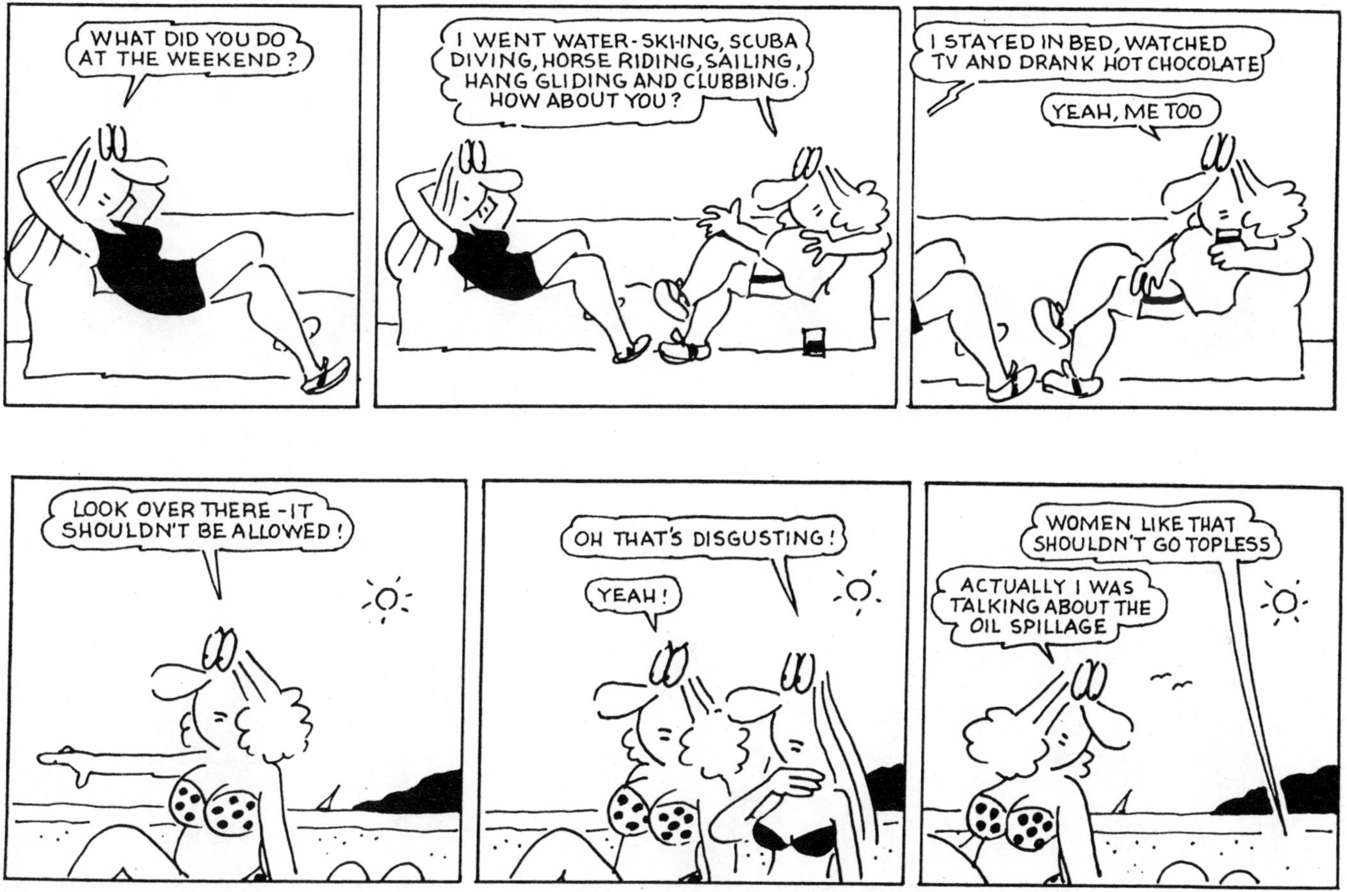
WHAT DID YOU DO AT THE WEEKEND?
I WENT WATER-SKI-ING, SCUBA DIVING, HORSE RIDING, SAILING, HANG GLIDING AND CLUBBING. HOW ABOUT YOU?
I STAYED IN BED, WATCHED TV AND DRANK HOT CHOCOLATE
YEAH, ME TOO
LOOK OVER THERE - IT SHOULDN'T BE ALLOWED!
OH THAT'S DISGUSTING!
YEAH!
WOMEN LIKE THAT SHOULDN'T GO TOPLESS
ACTUALLY I WAS TALKING ABOUT THE OIL SPILLAGE

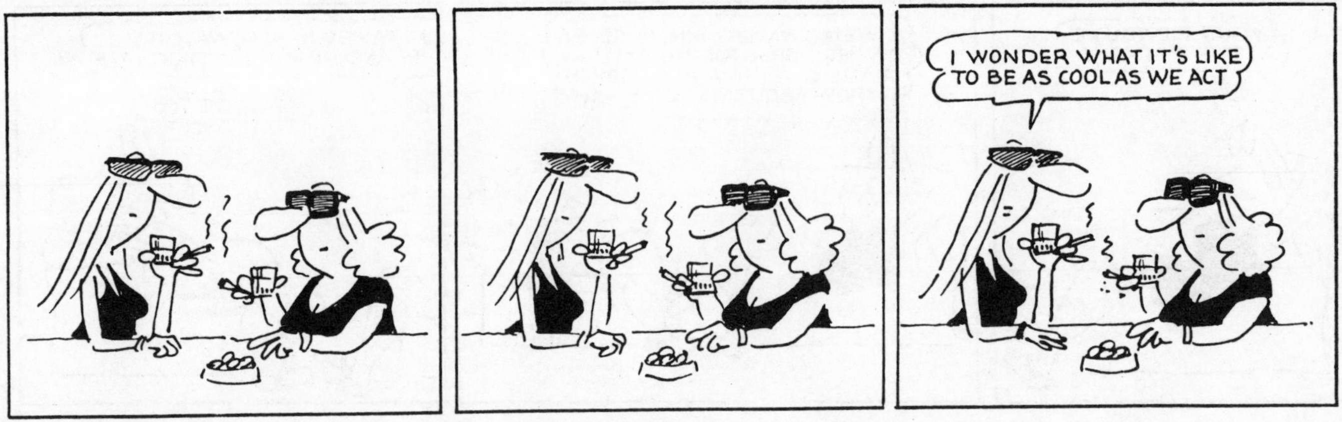
I WONDER WHAT IT'S LIKE TO BE AS COOL AS WE ACT

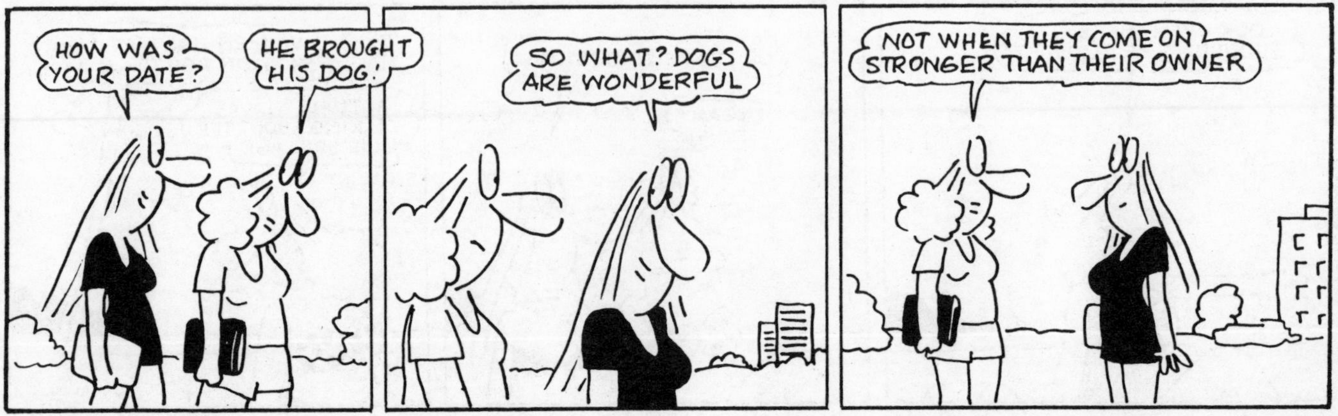
HOW WAS YOUR DATE?
HE BROUGHT HIS DOG!
SO WHAT? DOGS ARE WONDERFUL
NOT WHEN THEY COME ON STRONGER THAN THEIR OWNER

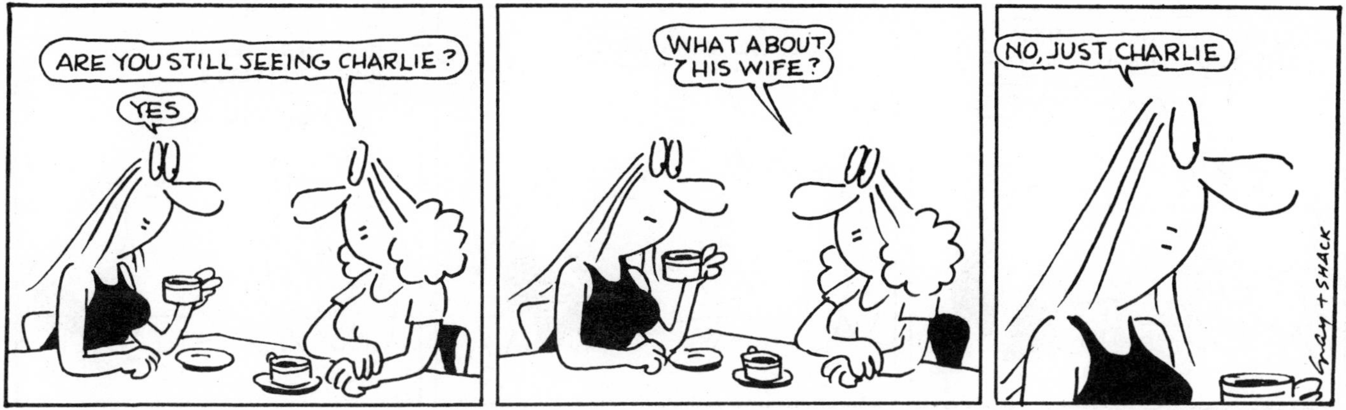
ARE YOU STILL SEEING CHARLIE?
YES
WHAT ABOUT HIS WIFE?
NO, JUST CHARLIE
Gray + SHACK

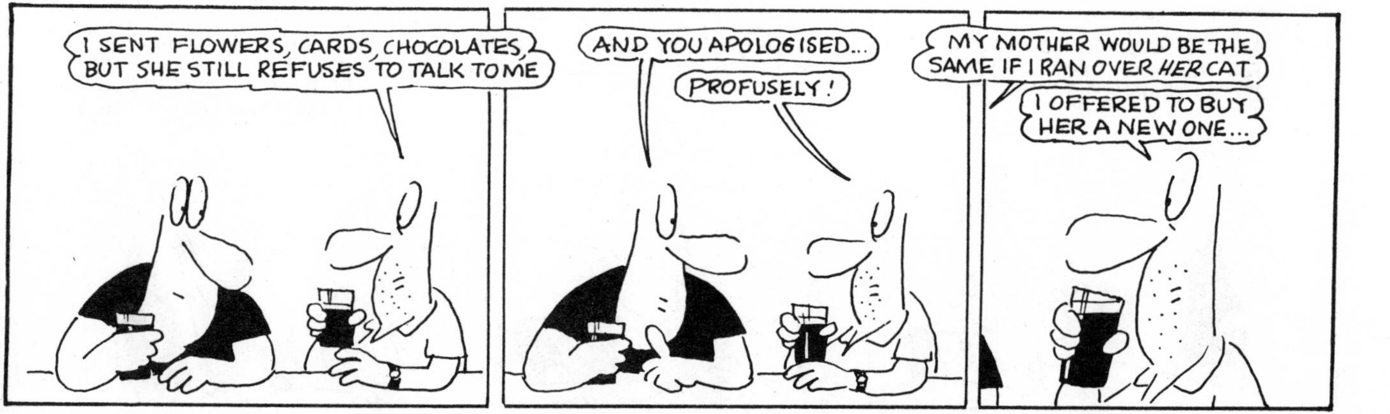
I SENT FLOWERS, CARDS, CHOCOLATES, BUT SHE STILL REFUSES TO TALK TO ME
AND YOU APOLOGISED...
PROFUSELY!
MY MOTHER WOULD BE THE SAME IF I RAN OVER HER CAT
I OFFERED TO BUY HER A NEW ONE...

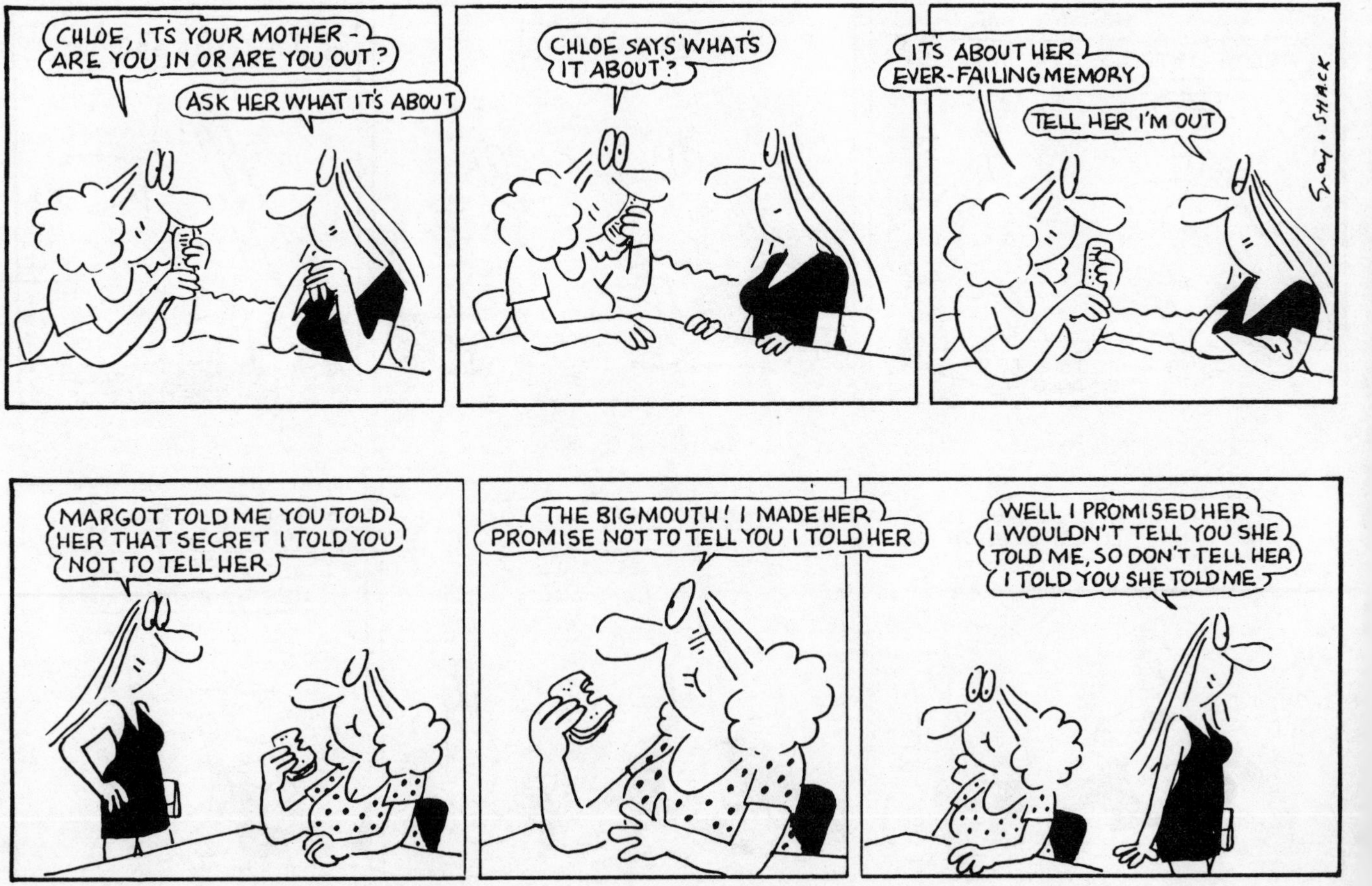
CHLOE, IT'S YOUR MOTHER - ARE YOU IN OR ARE YOU OUT?
ASK HER WHAT IT'S ABOUT
CHLOE SAYS 'WHAT'S IT ABOUT'?
IT'S ABOUT HER EVER-FAILING MEMORY
TELL HER I'M OUT
MARGOT TOLD ME YOU TOLD HER THAT SECRET I TOLD YOU NOT TO TELL HER
THE BIGMOUTH! I MADE HER PROMISE NOT TO TELL YOU I TOLD HER
WELL I PROMISED HER I WOULDN'T TELL YOU SHE TOLD ME, SO DON'T TELL HER I TOLD YOU SHE TOLD ME

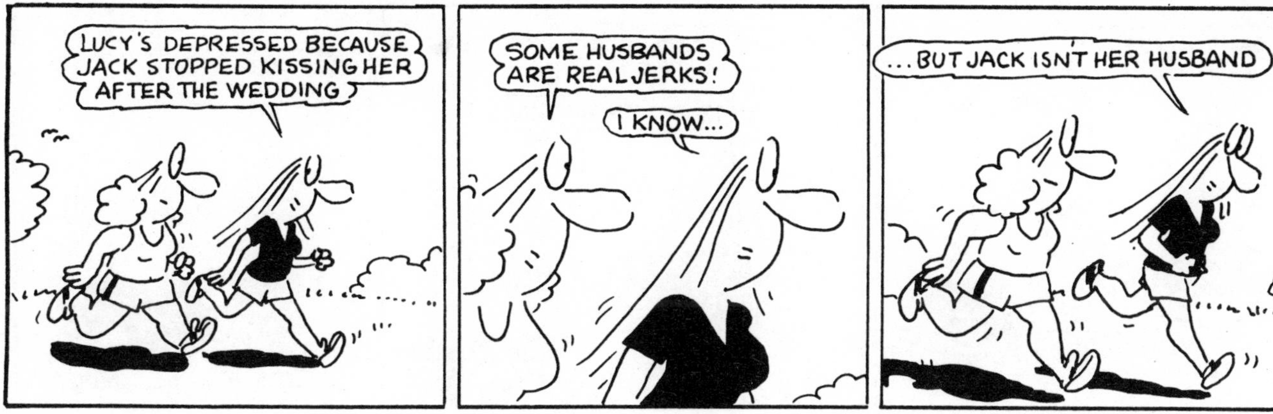
LUCY'S DEPRESSED BECAUSE JACK STOPPED KISSING HER AFTER THE WEDDING
SOME HUSBANDS ARE REAL JERKS!
I KNOW...
...BUT JACK ISN'T HER HUSBAND

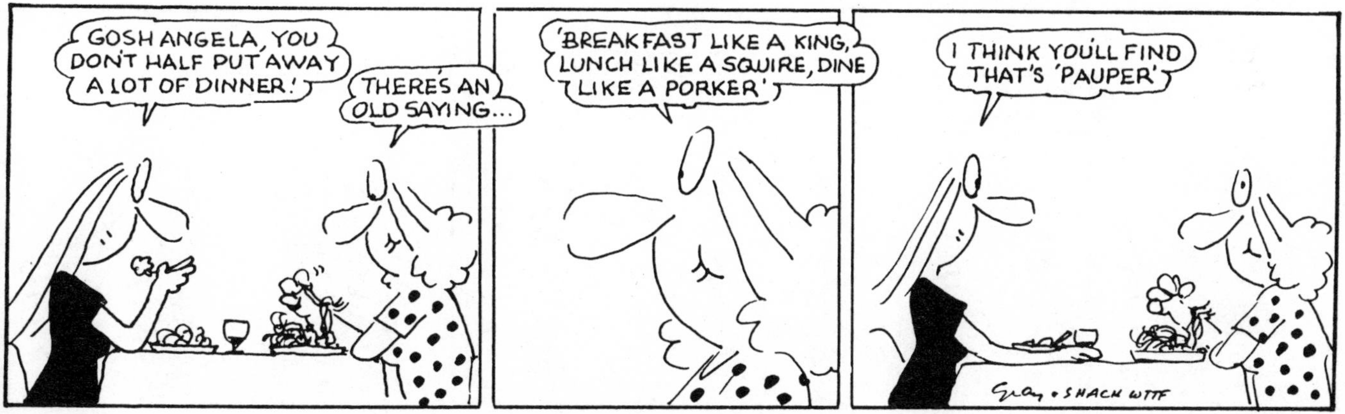
GOSH ANGELA, YOU DON'T HALF PUT AWAY A LOT OF DINNER!
THERE'S AN OLD SAYING...
'BREAKFAST LIKE A KING, LUNCH LIKE A SQUIRE, DINE LIKE A PORKER'
I THINK YOU'LL FIND THAT'S 'PAUPER'

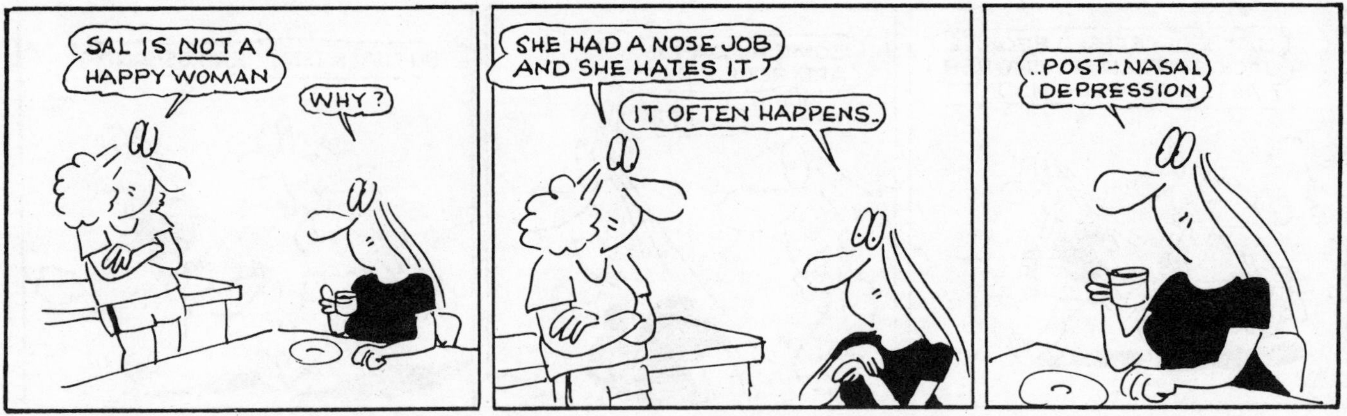
SAL IS NOT A HAPPY WOMAN
WHY?
SHE HAD A NOSE JOB AND SHE HATES IT
IT OFTEN HAPPENS..
..POST-NASAL DEPRESSION

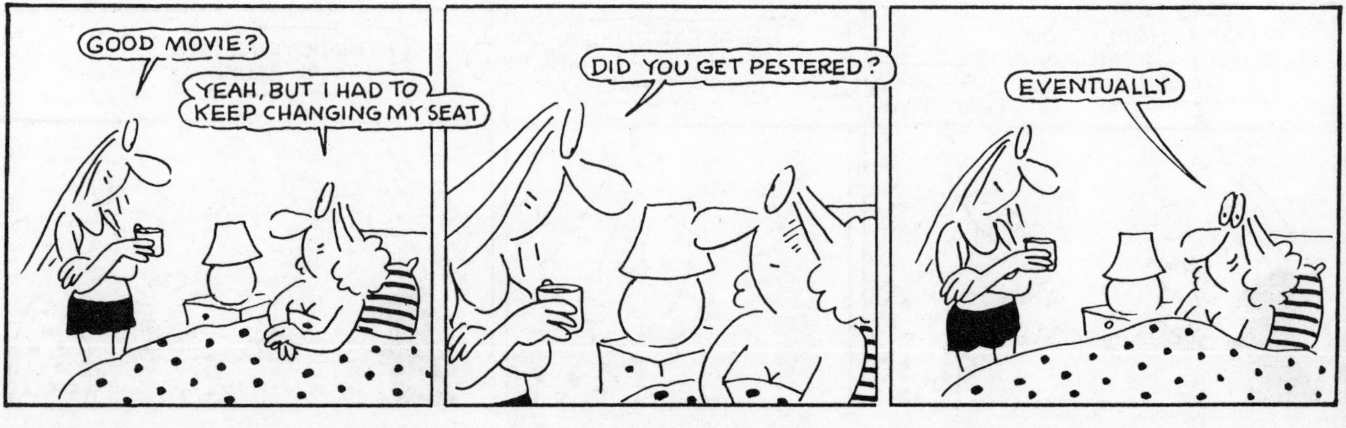
GOOD MOVIE?
YEAH, BUT I HAD TO KEEP CHANGING MY SEAT
DID YOU GET PESTERED?
EVENTUALLY

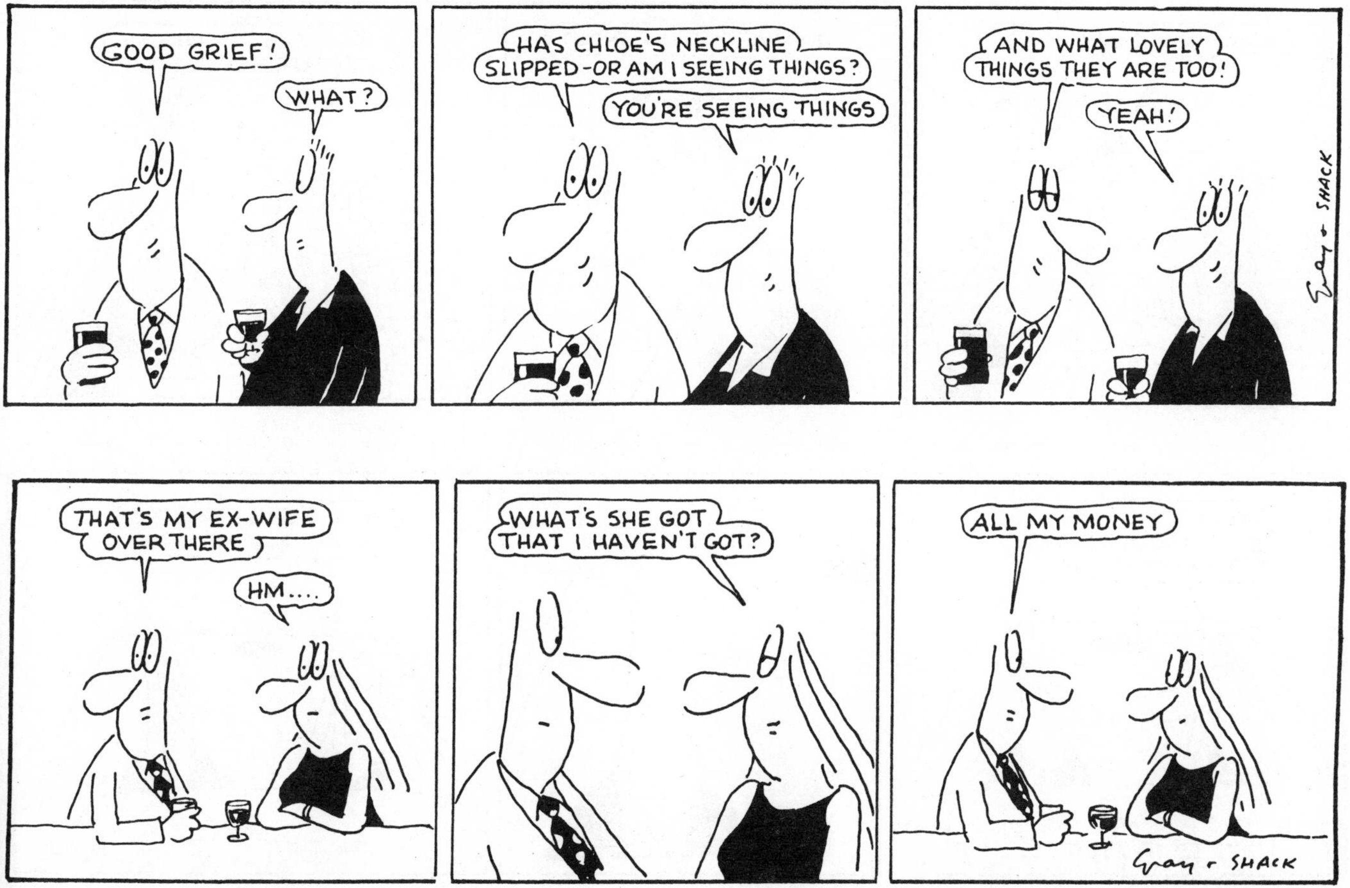

GOOD GRIEF!
WHAT?
HAS CHLOE'S NECKLINE SLIPPED-OR AM I SEEING THINGS?
YOU'RE SEEING THINGS
AND WHAT LOVELY THINGS THEY ARE TOO!
YEAH!
Gray + SHACK
THAT'S MY EX-WIFE OVER THERE
HM....
WHAT'S SHE GOT THAT I HAVEN'T GOT?
ALL MY MONEY
Gray + SHACK

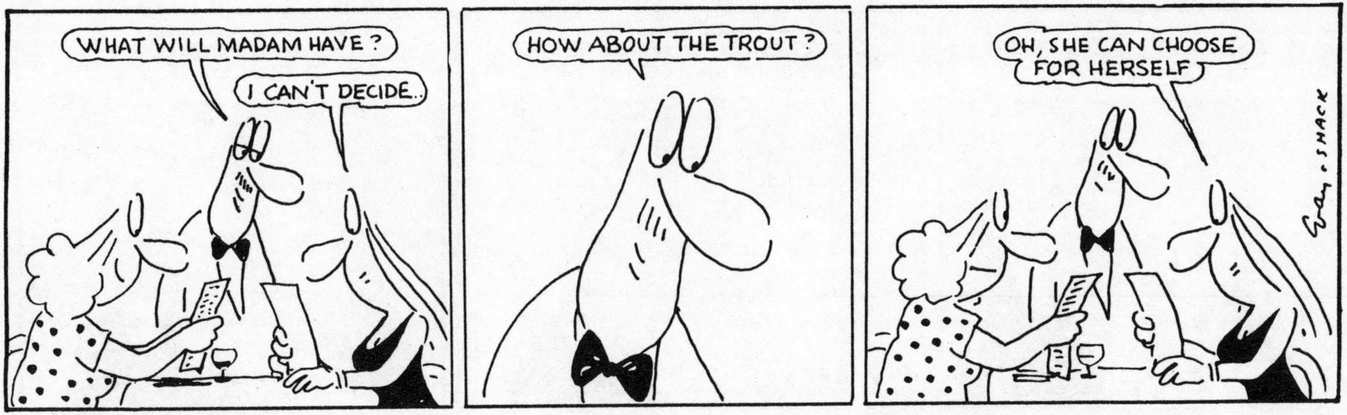
WHAT WILL MADAM HAVE?
I CAN'T DECIDE..
HOW ABOUT THE TROUT?
OH, SHE CAN CHOOSE FOR HERSELF

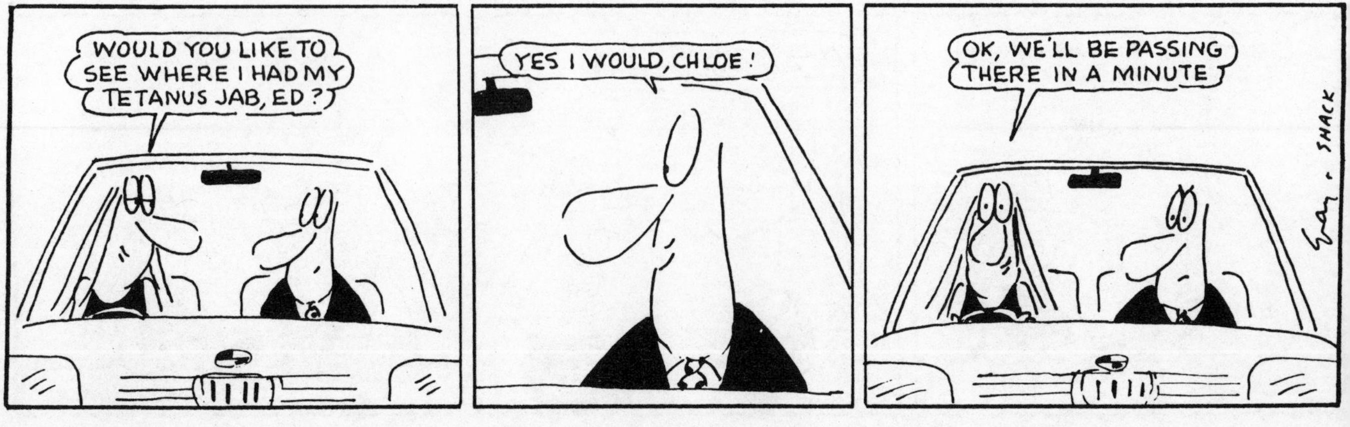
WOULD YOU LIKE TO SEE WHERE I HAD MY TETANUS JAB, ED?
YES I WOULD, CHLOE!
OK, WE'LL BE PASSING THERE IN A MINUTE

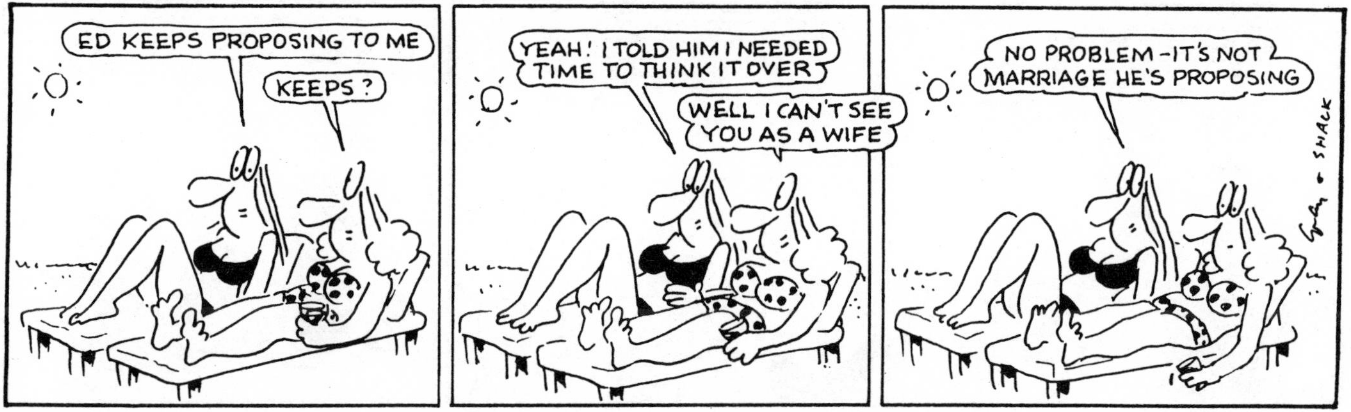
ED KEEPS PROPOSING TO ME
KEEPS ?
YEAH! I TOLD HIM I NEEDED TIME TO THINK IT OVER
WELL I CAN'T SEE YOU AS A WIFE
NO PROBLEM - IT'S NOT MARRIAGE HE'S PROPOSING
SHACK

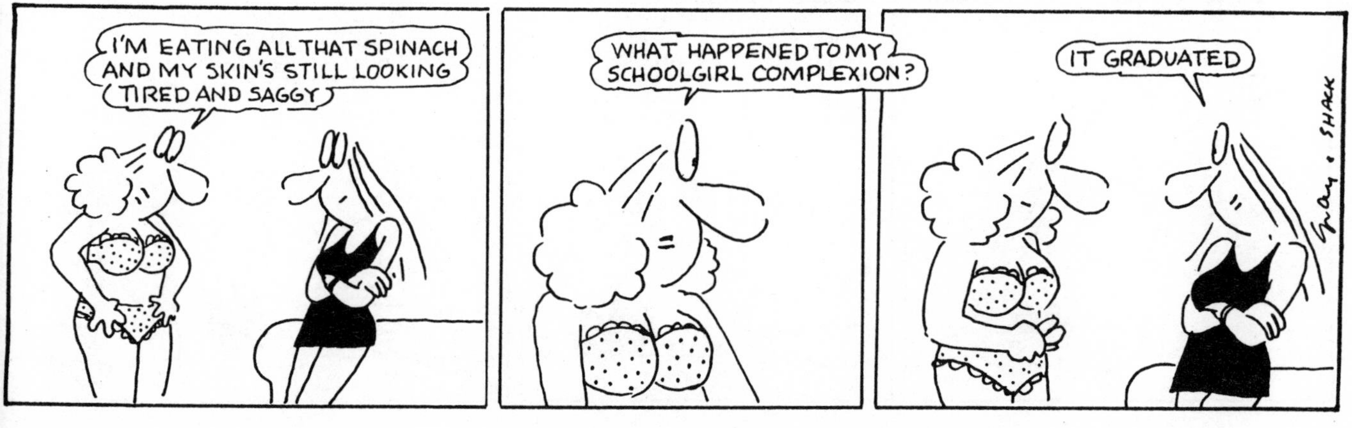
I'M EATING ALL THAT SPINACH AND MY SKIN'S STILL LOOKING TIRED AND SAGGY
WHAT HAPPENED TO MY SCHOOLGIRL COMPLEXION?
IT GRADUATED
SHACK

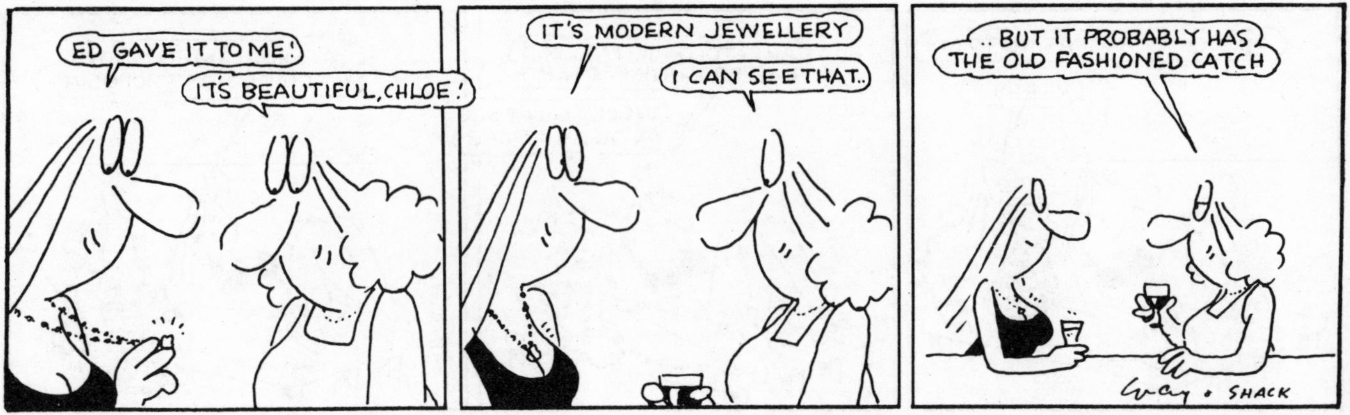
ED GAVE IT TO ME!
IT'S BEAUTIFUL, CHLOE!
IT'S MODERN JEWELLERY
I CAN SEE THAT..
.. BUT IT PROBABLY HAS THE OLD FASHIONED CATCH

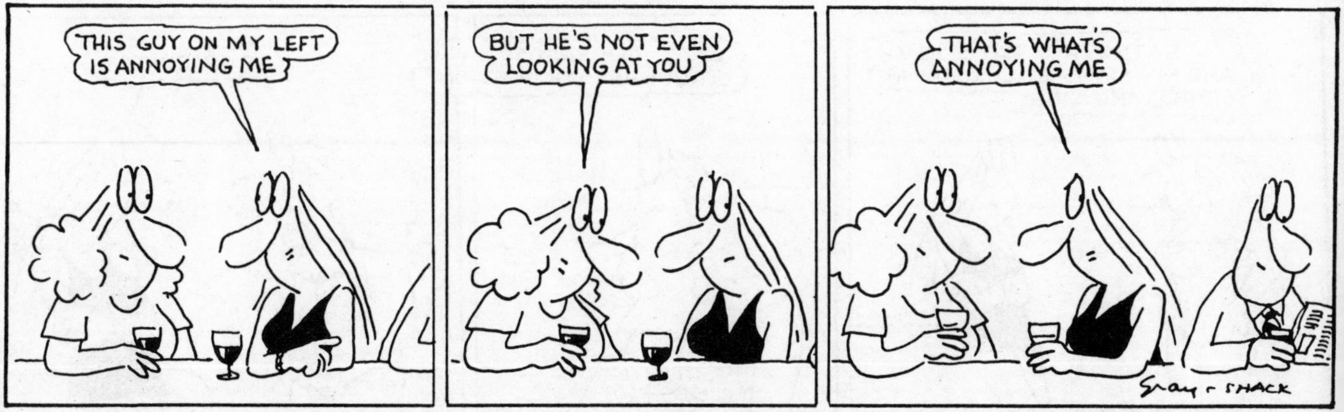
THIS GUY ON MY LEFT IS ANNOYING ME
BUT HE'S NOT EVEN LOOKING AT YOU
THAT'S WHATS ANNOYING ME

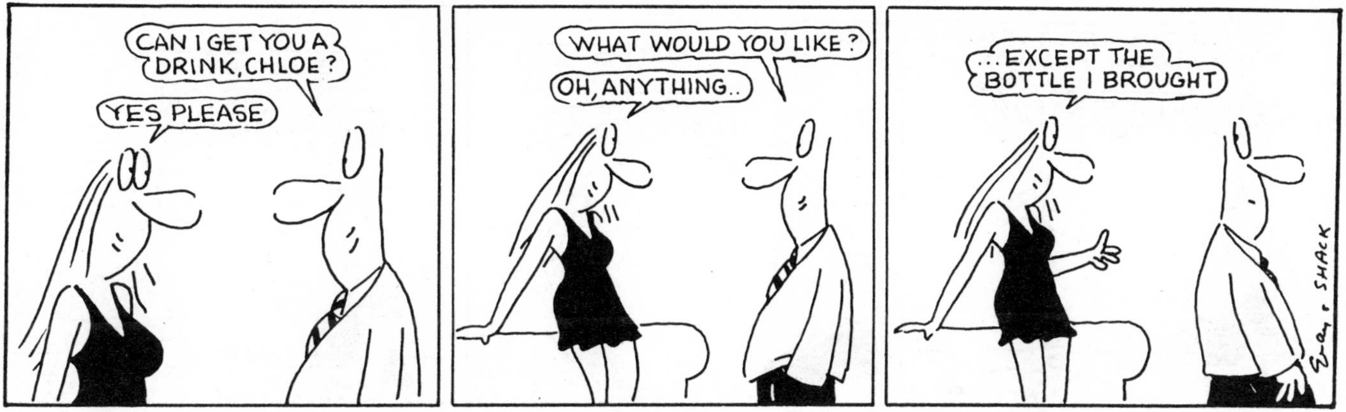
CAN I GET YOU A DRINK, CHLOE?
YES PLEASE
WHAT WOULD YOU LIKE?
OH, ANYTHING..
...EXCEPT THE BOTTLE I BROUGHT

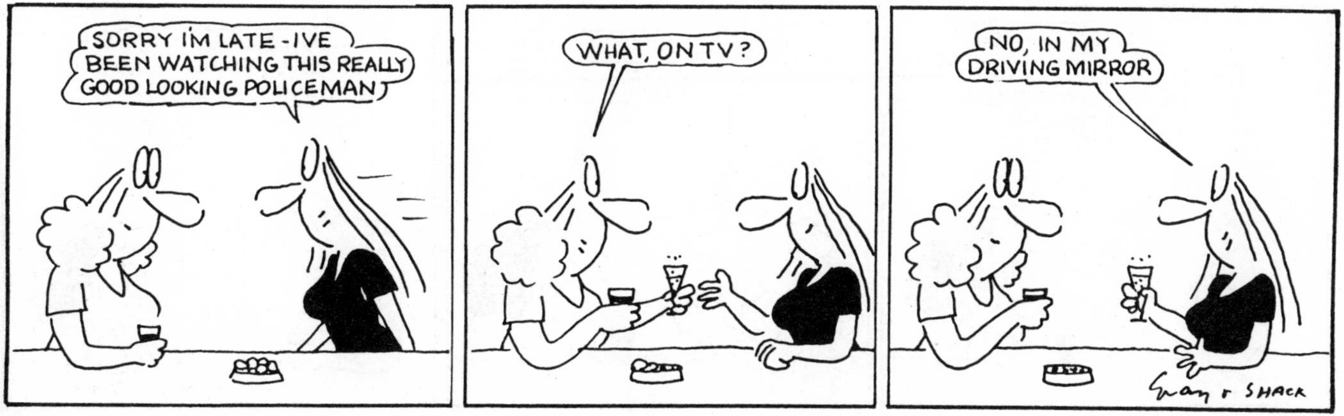
SORRY I'M LATE - IVE BEEN WATCHING THIS REALLY GOOD LOOKING POLICEMAN
WHAT, ON TV?
NO, IN MY DRIVING MIRROR

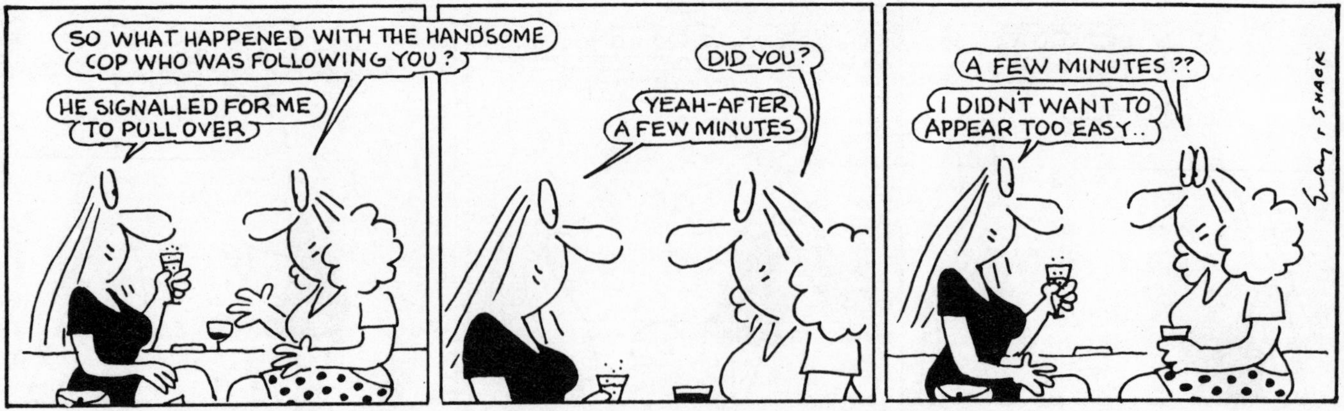
SO WHAT HAPPENED WITH THE HANDSOME COP WHO WAS FOLLOWING YOU ?
HE SIGNALLED FOR ME TO PULL OVER
DID YOU ?
YEAH-AFTER A FEW MINUTES
A FEW MINUTES ??
I DIDN'T WANT TO APPEAR TOO EASY..
Evans & SHACK

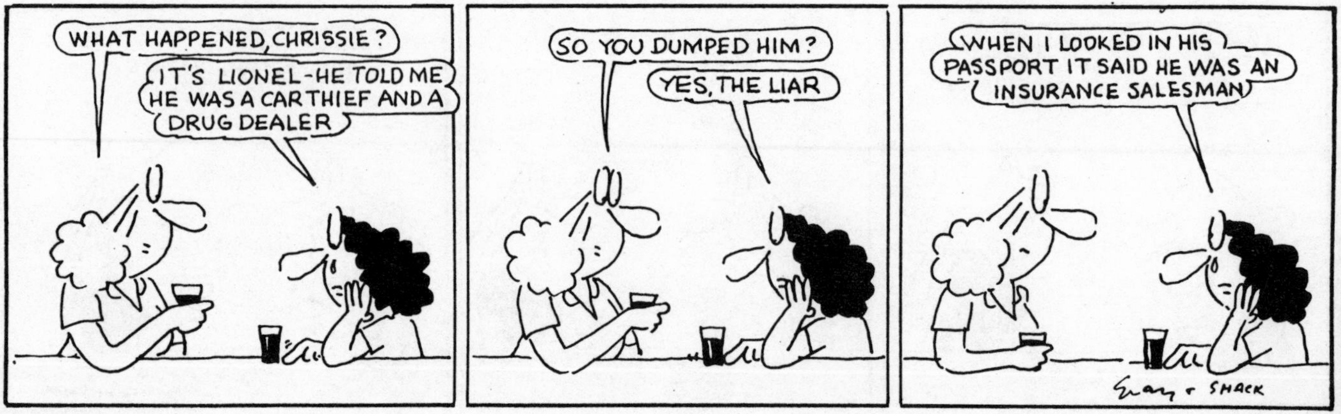
WHAT HAPPENED, CHRISSIE ?
IT'S LIONEL-HE TOLD ME HE WAS A CAR THIEF AND A DRUG DEALER
SO YOU DUMPED HIM ?
YES, THE LIAR
WHEN I LOOKED IN HIS PASSPORT IT SAID HE WAS AN INSURANCE SALESMAN
Evans & SHACK

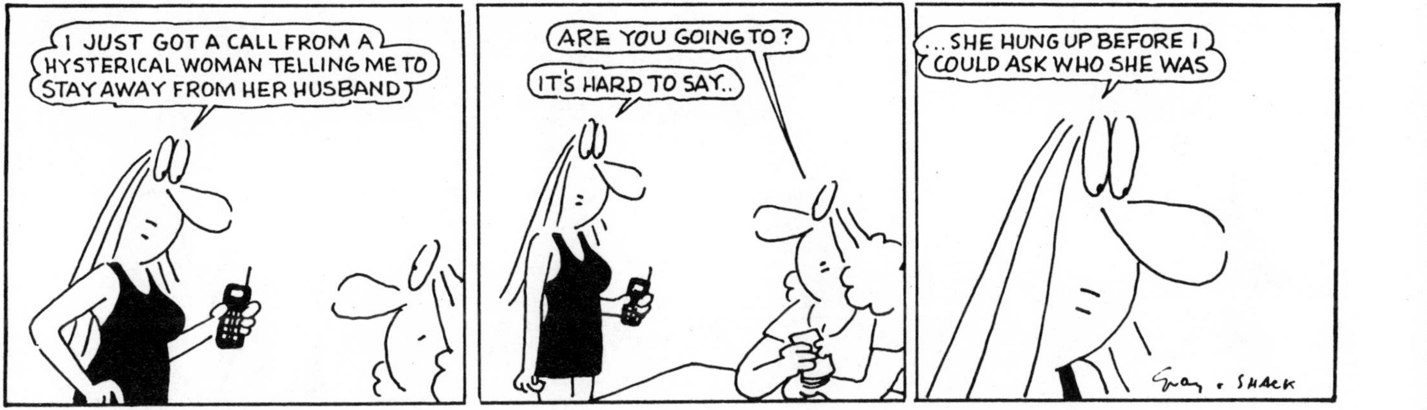
I JUST GOT A CALL FROM A HYSTERICAL WOMAN TELLING ME TO STAY AWAY FROM HER HUSBAND
ARE YOU GOING TO?
IT'S HARD TO SAY..
...SHE HUNG UP BEFORE I COULD ASK WHO SHE WAS

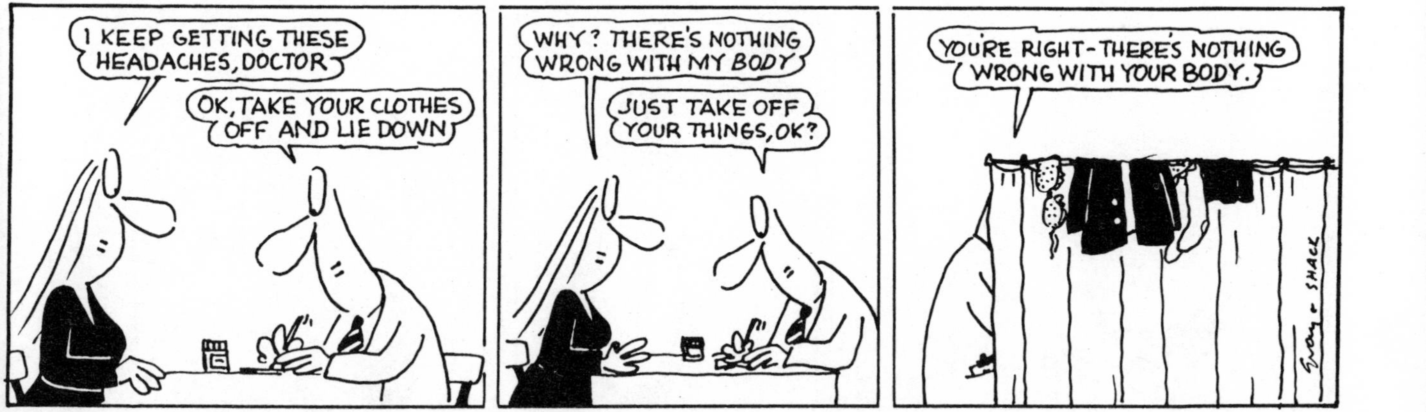
I KEEP GETTING THESE HEADACHES, DOCTOR
OK, TAKE YOUR CLOTHES OFF AND LIE DOWN
WHY? THERE'S NOTHING WRONG WITH MY BODY
JUST TAKE OFF YOUR THINGS, OK?
YOU'RE RIGHT - THERE'S NOTHING WRONG WITH YOUR BODY.

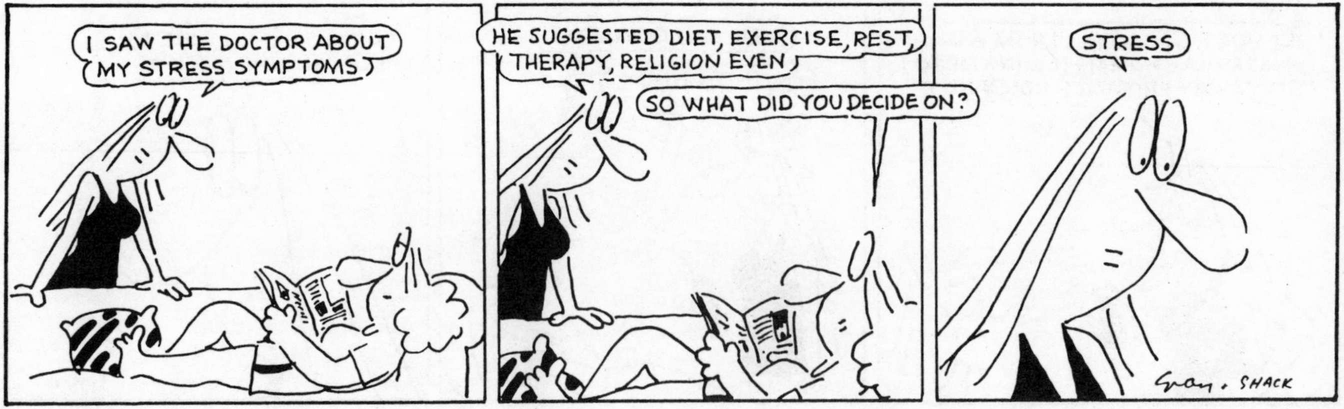
I SAW THE DOCTOR ABOUT MY STRESS SYMPTOMS
HE SUGGESTED DIET, EXERCISE, REST, THERAPY, RELIGION EVEN
SO WHAT DID YOU DECIDE ON?
STRESS
Gray • SHACK

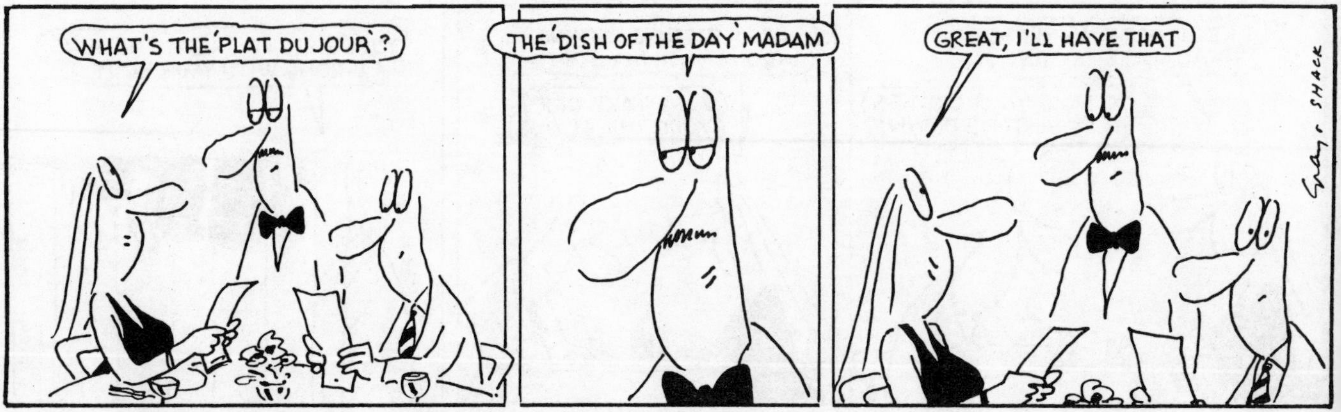
WHAT'S THE 'PLAT DU JOUR'?
THE 'DISH OF THE DAY' MADAM
GREAT, I'LL HAVE THAT
Gray • SHACK

LOOK AT CHLOE - AFTER MAKING A SPECTACLE OF HERSELF LAST NIGHT YOU'D THINK SHE'D GO INTO HIDING...
BUT NO - THERE SHE IS AGAIN REPEATING THE WHOLE SORRY EPISODE!
NOT EXACTLY..
..THAT'S A DIFFERENT GUY

I'M IMPRESSED! I HAD NO IDEA YOU WERE A MAGICIAN
I'M NOT - WHAT MAKES YOU SAY THAT?
YOU JUST TURNED THE RUG INTO AN ASHTRAY

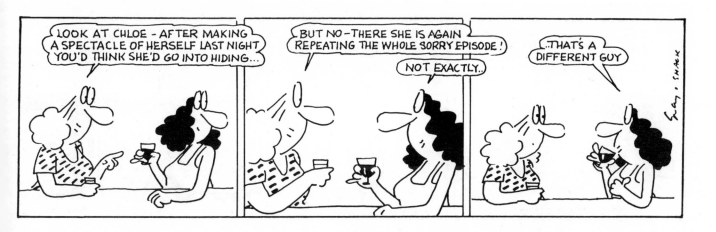

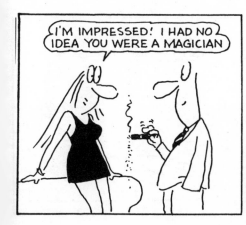

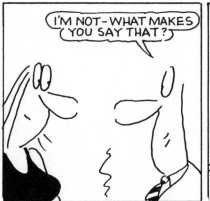

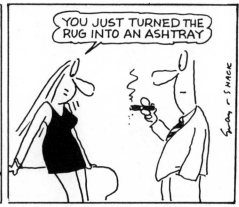

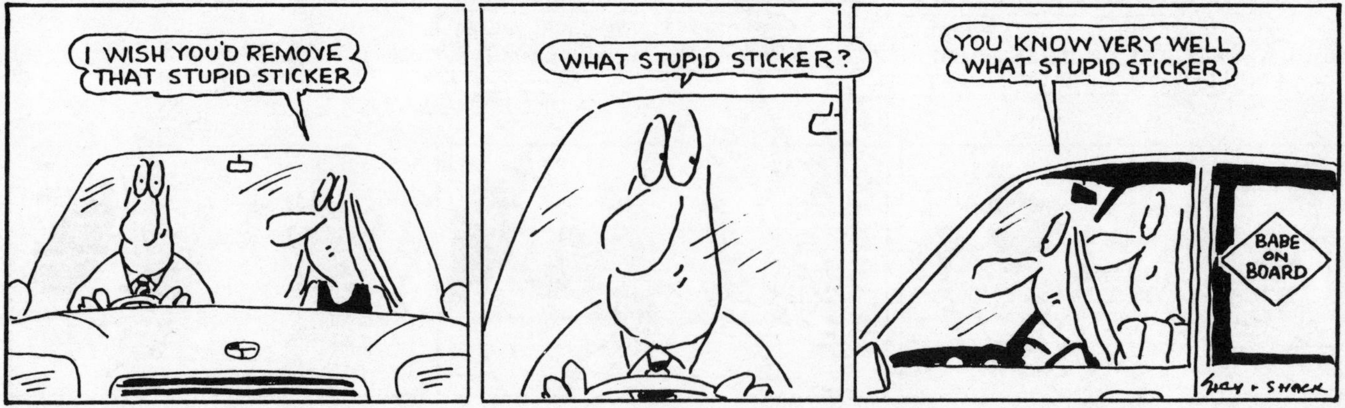
I WISH YOU'D REMOVE THAT STUPID STICKER
WHAT STUPID STICKER?
YOU KNOW VERY WELL WHAT STUPID STICKER
BABE ON BOARD

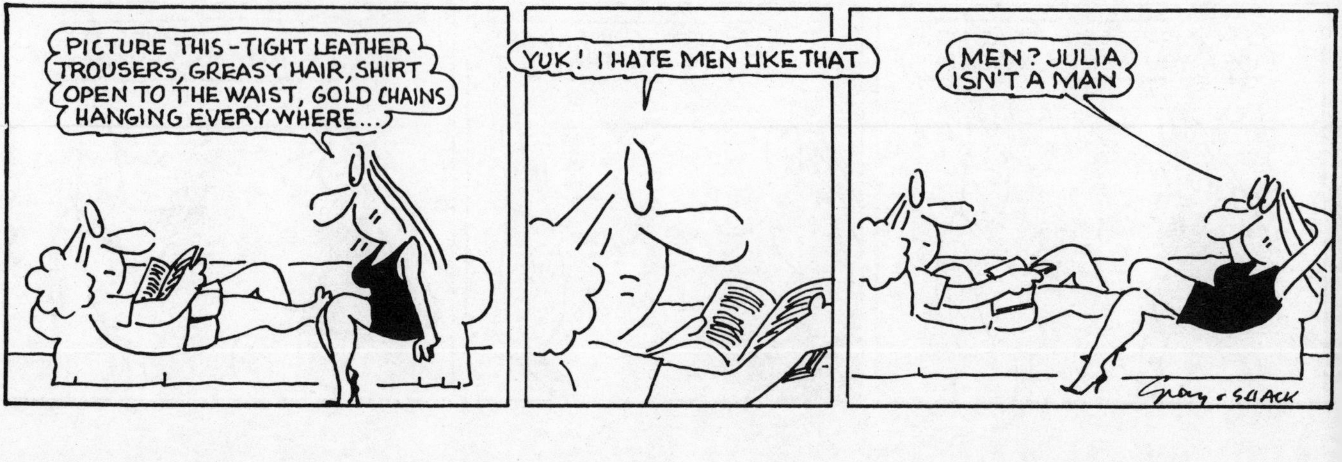
PICTURE THIS - TIGHT LEATHER TROUSERS, GREASY HAIR, SHIRT OPEN TO THE WAIST, GOLD CHAINS HANGING EVERY WHERE...
YUK! I HATE MEN LIKE THAT
MEN? JULIA ISN'T A MAN

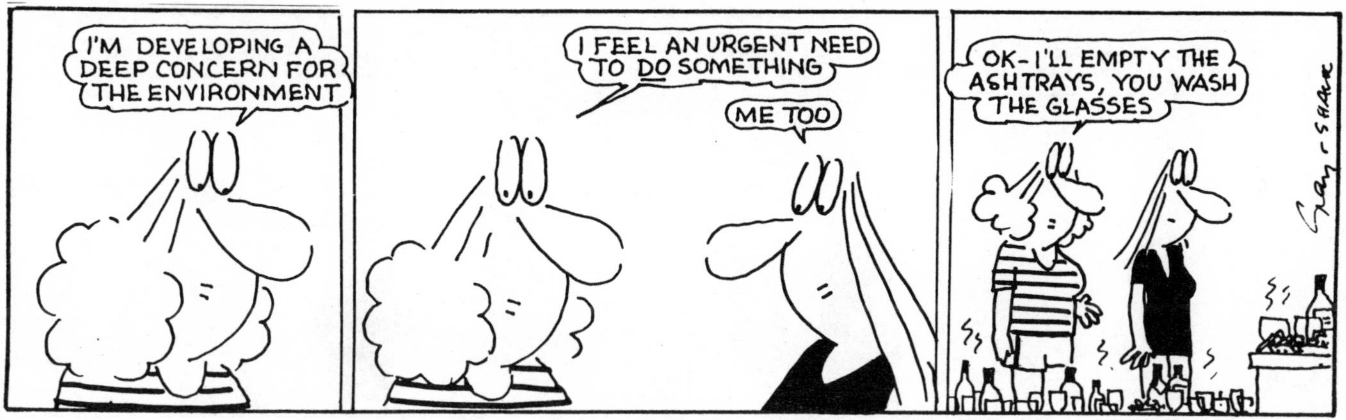
I'M DEVELOPING A DEEP CONCERN FOR THE ENVIRONMENT
I FEEL AN URGENT NEED TO DO SOMETHING
ME TOO
OK - I'LL EMPTY THE ASHTRAYS, YOU WASH THE GLASSES

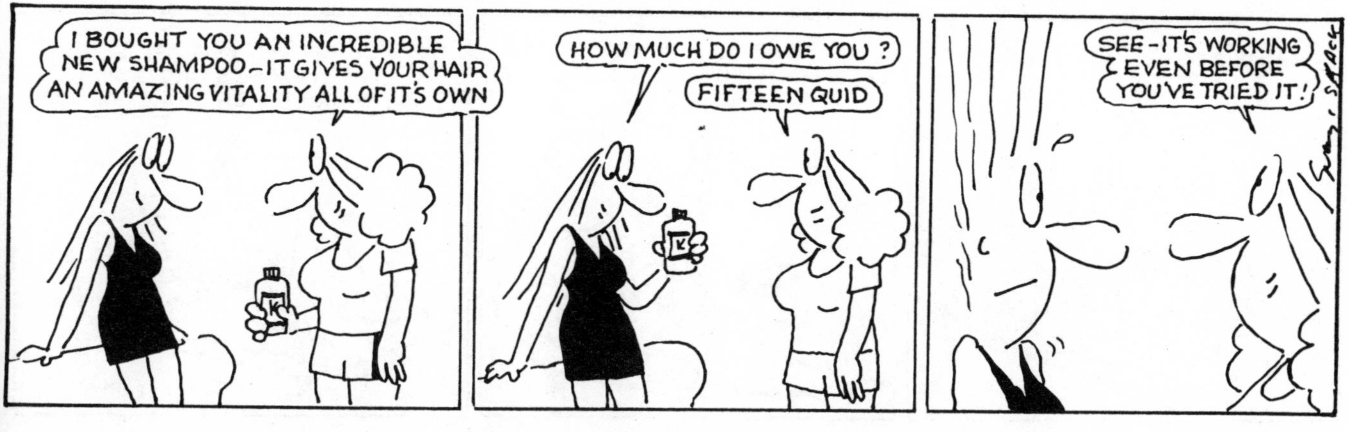
I BOUGHT YOU AN INCREDIBLE NEW SHAMPOO - IT GIVES YOUR HAIR AN AMAZING VITALITY ALL OF IT'S OWN
HOW MUCH DO I OWE YOU ?
FIFTEEN QUID
SEE - IT'S WORKING EVEN BEFORE YOU'VE TRIED IT !

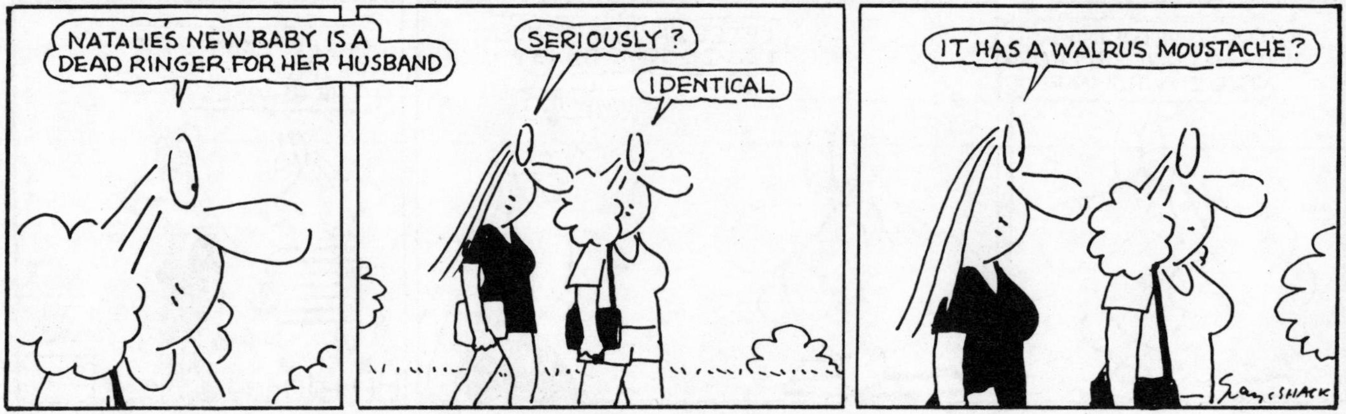
NATALIE'S NEW BABY IS A DEAD RINGER FOR HER HUSBAND
SERIOUSLY?
IDENTICAL
IT HAS A WALRUS MOUSTACHE?

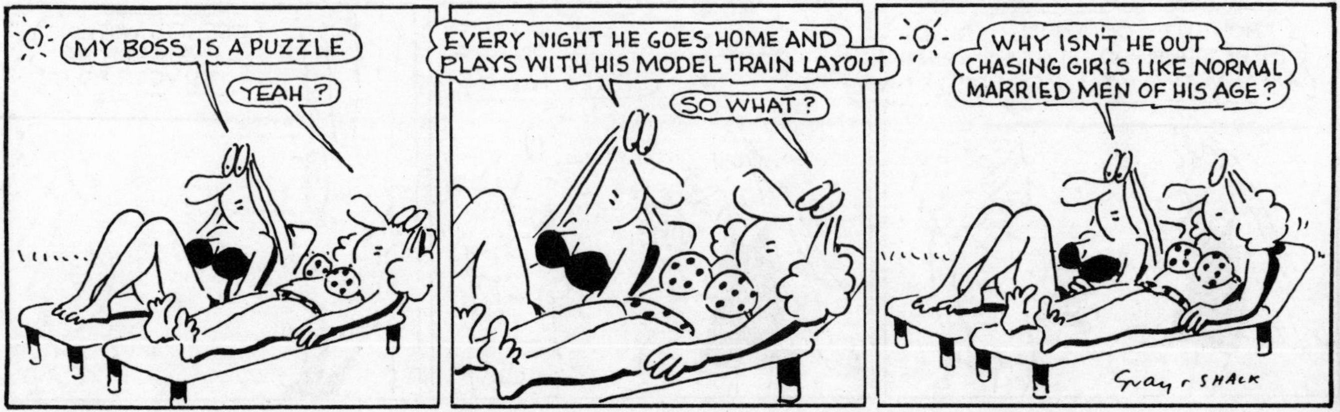
MY BOSS IS A PUZZLE
YEAH?
EVERY NIGHT HE GOES HOME AND PLAYS WITH HIS MODEL TRAIN LAYOUT
SO WHAT?
WHY ISN'T HE OUT CHASING GIRLS LIKE NORMAL MARRIED MEN OF HIS AGE?

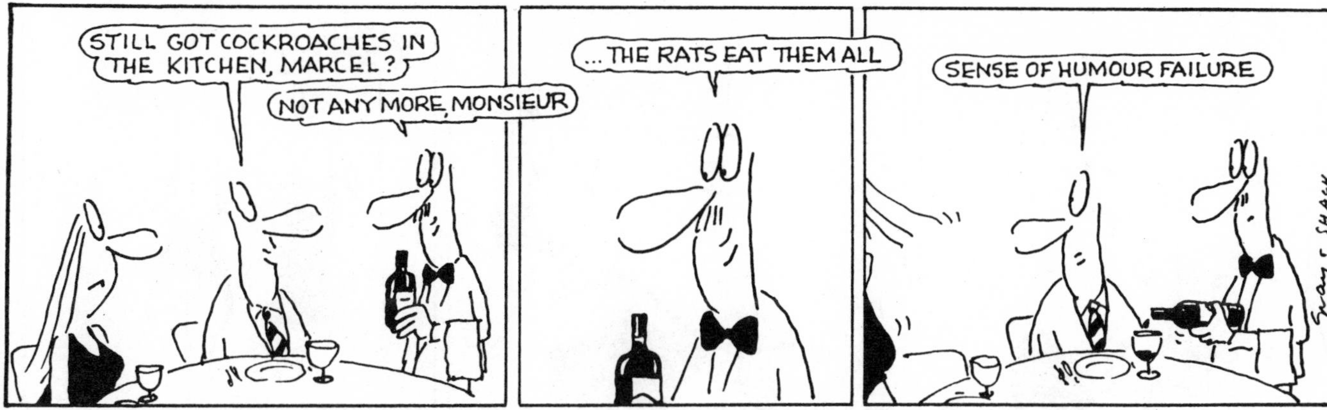
STILL GOT COCKROACHES IN THE KITCHEN, MARCEL?
NOT ANY MORE, MONSIEUR
... THE RATS EAT THEM ALL
SENSE OF HUMOUR FAILURE

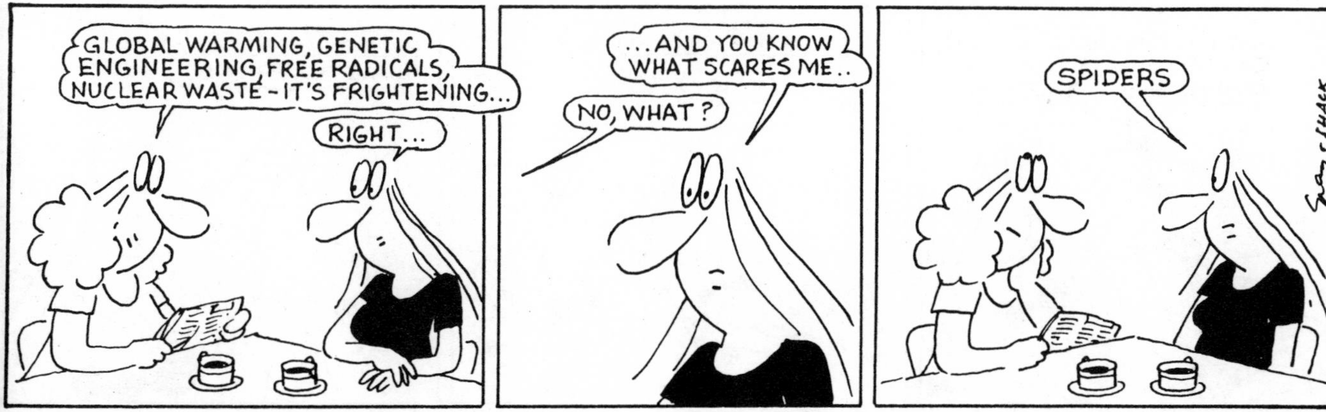
GLOBAL WARMING, GENETIC ENGINEERING, FREE RADICALS, NUCLEAR WASTE - IT'S FRIGHTENING...
RIGHT...
...AND YOU KNOW WHAT SCARES ME..
NO, WHAT?
SPIDERS

PERFECT!

WHY IS IT SO HARD TO FIND A MAN WHO IS SENSITIVE, CARING AND GOOD LOOKING?
THAT'S AN EASY ONE
IT IS?
YES - THEY ALREADY HAVE BOYFRIENDS

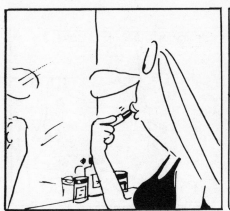

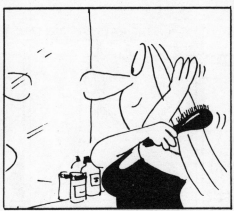

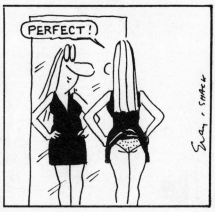

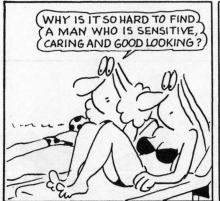

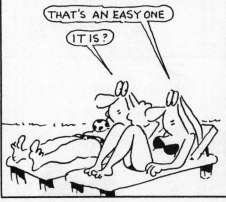

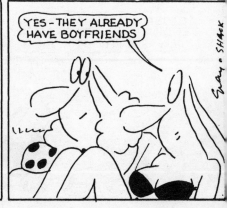

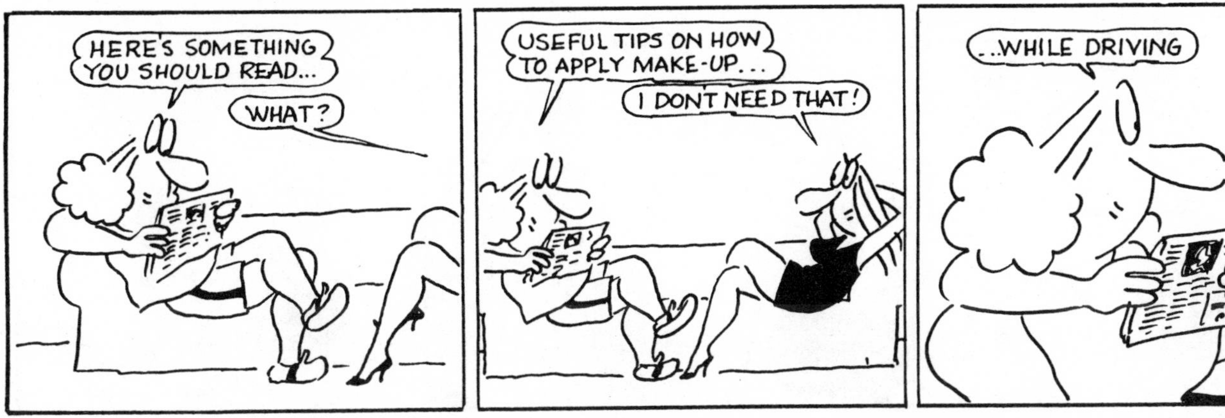
HERE'S SOMETHING YOU SHOULD READ...
WHAT?
USEFUL TIPS ON HOW TO APPLY MAKE-UP...
I DON'T NEED THAT!
...WHILE DRIVING

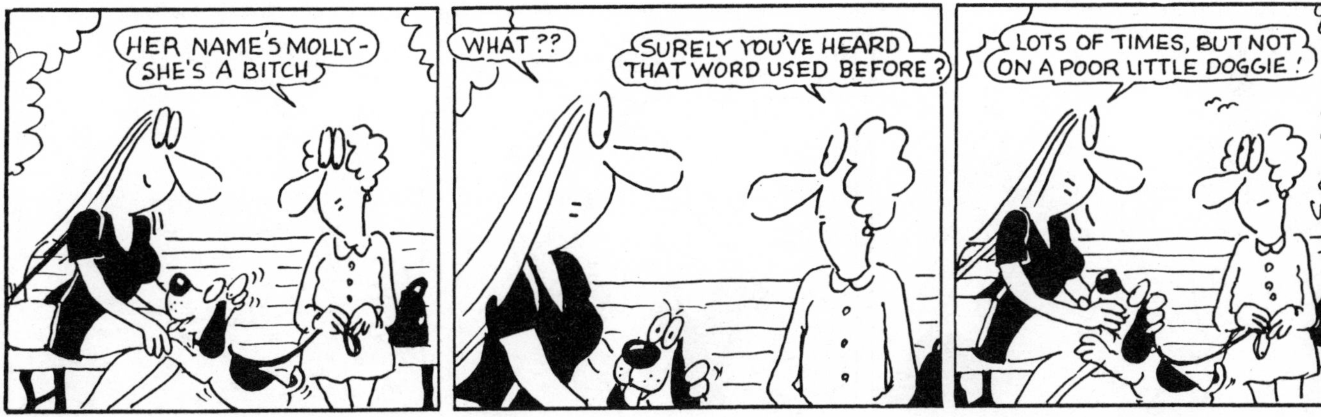
HER NAME'S MOLLY- SHE'S A BITCH
WHAT??
SURELY YOU'VE HEARD THAT WORD USED BEFORE?
LOTS OF TIMES, BUT NOT ON A POOR LITTLE DOGGIE!

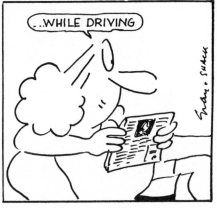

DON'T YOU JUST LOVE THINKING ABOUT THE PAST?
WHY?
WELL, IT BRINGS BACK SO MANY MEMORIES!
SHACK

BE CAREFUL WHEN YOU SIT ON THAT COUCH
WHY?
IF YOU PUSH DOWN ON BOTH ARMS AND PRESS THE BACK IT TURNS INTO A BED
I SEE WHAT YOU MEAN
SHACK

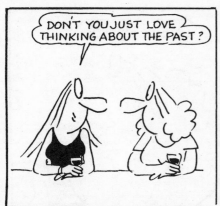

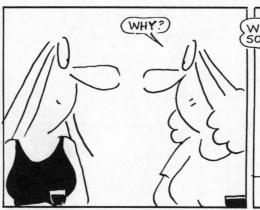

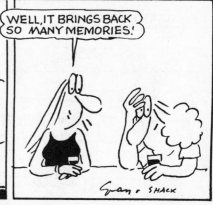

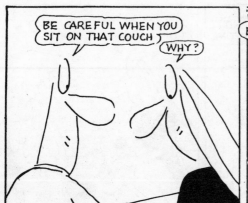

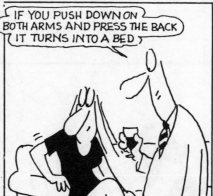

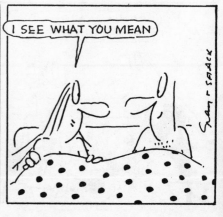

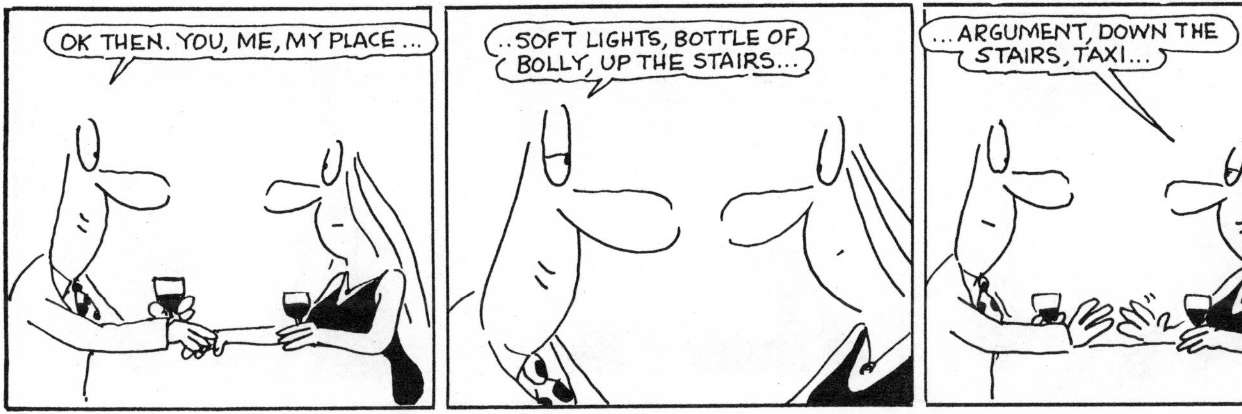
OK THEN. YOU, ME, MY PLACE...
..SOFT LIGHTS, BOTTLE OF BOLLY, UP THE STAIRS...
...ARGUMENT, DOWN THE STAIRS, TAXI...

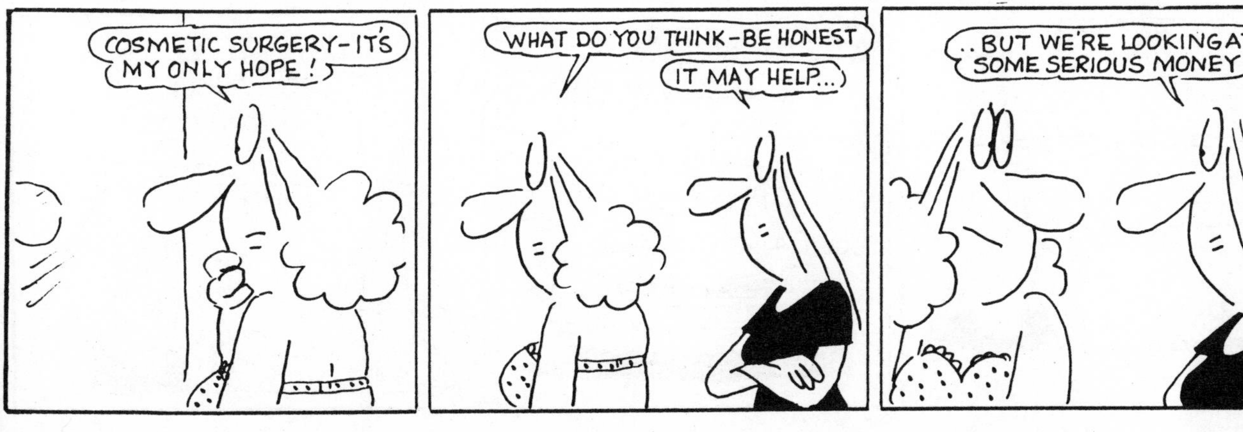
COSMETIC SURGERY-IT'S MY ONLY HOPE!
WHAT DO YOU THINK-BE HONEST
IT MAY HELP...
..BUT WE'RE LOOKINGAT SOME SERIOUS MONEY

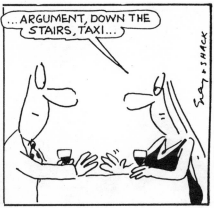

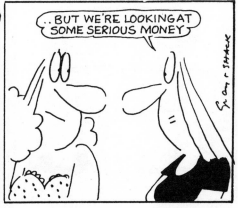

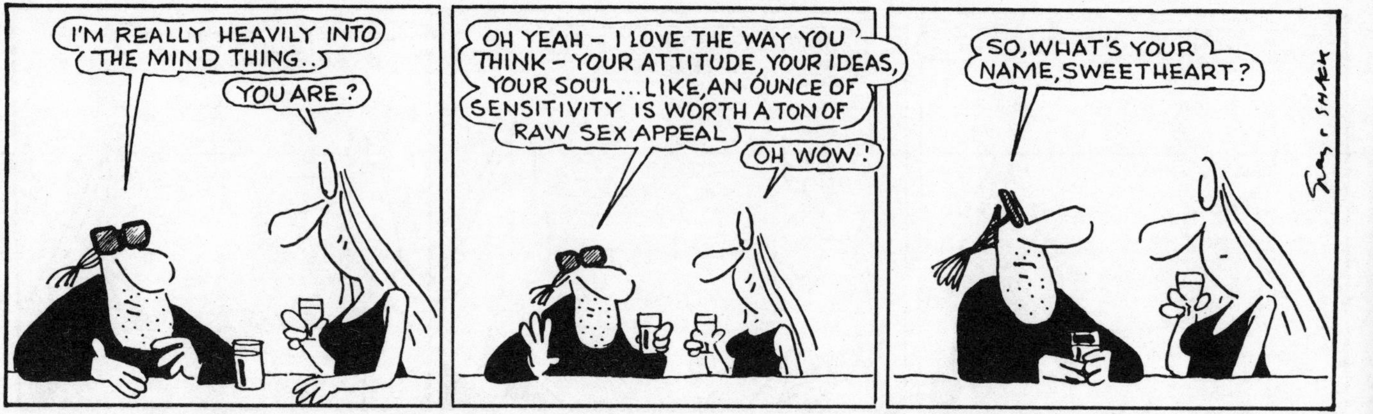
I'M REALLY HEAVILY INTO THE MIND THING..
YOU ARE ?
OH YEAH – I LOVE THE WAY YOU THINK – YOUR ATTITUDE, YOUR IDEAS, YOUR SOUL... LIKE, AN OUNCE OF SENSITIVITY IS WORTH A TON OF RAW SEX APPEAL
OH WOW !
SO, WHAT'S YOUR NAME, SWEETHEART ?

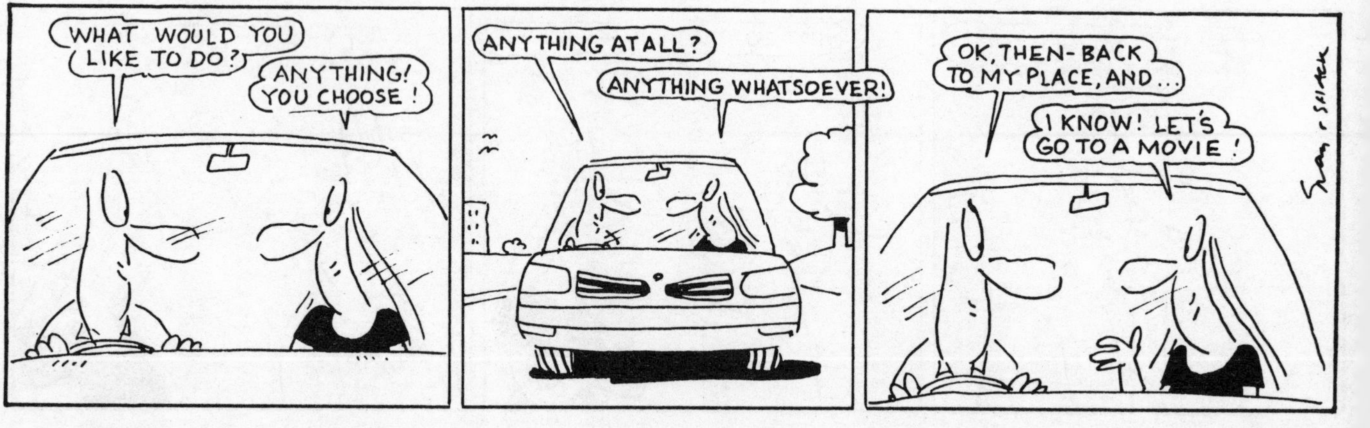
WHAT WOULD YOU LIKE TO DO ?
ANYTHING! YOU CHOOSE !
ANYTHING AT ALL ?
ANYTHING WHATSOEVER !
OK, THEN- BACK TO MY PLACE, AND...
I KNOW! LET'S GO TO A MOVIE !

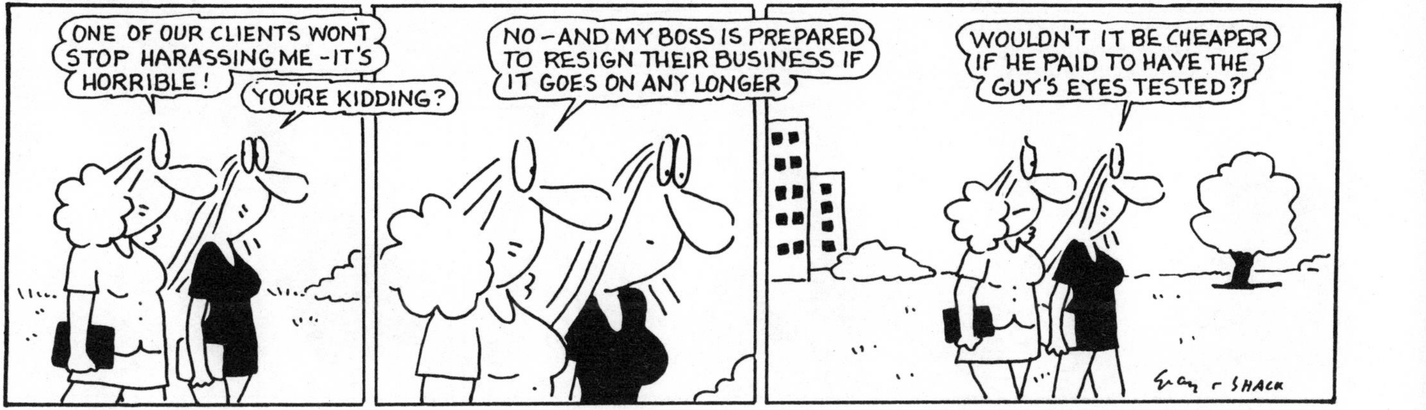
ONE OF OUR CLIENTS WON'T STOP HARASSING ME - IT'S HORRIBLE!
YOU'RE KIDDING?
NO - AND MY BOSS IS PREPARED TO RESIGN THEIR BUSINESS IF IT GOES ON ANY LONGER
WOULDN'T IT BE CHEAPER IF HE PAID TO HAVE THE GUY'S EYES TESTED?
SHACK

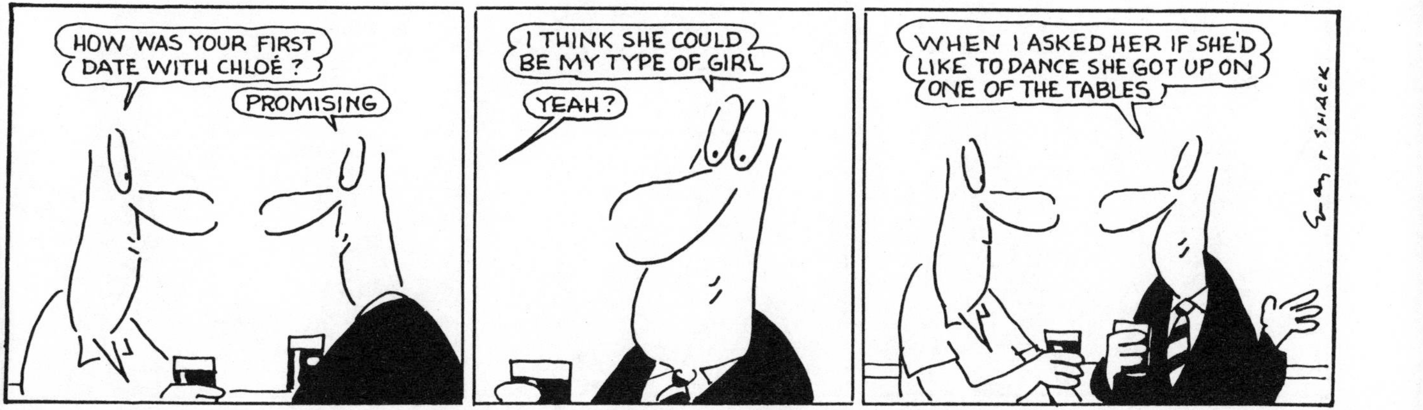
HOW WAS YOUR FIRST DATE WITH CHLOÉ?
PROMISING
I THINK SHE COULD BE MY TYPE OF GIRL
YEAH?
WHEN I ASKED HER IF SHE'D LIKE TO DANCE SHE GOT UP ON ONE OF THE TABLES
SHACK

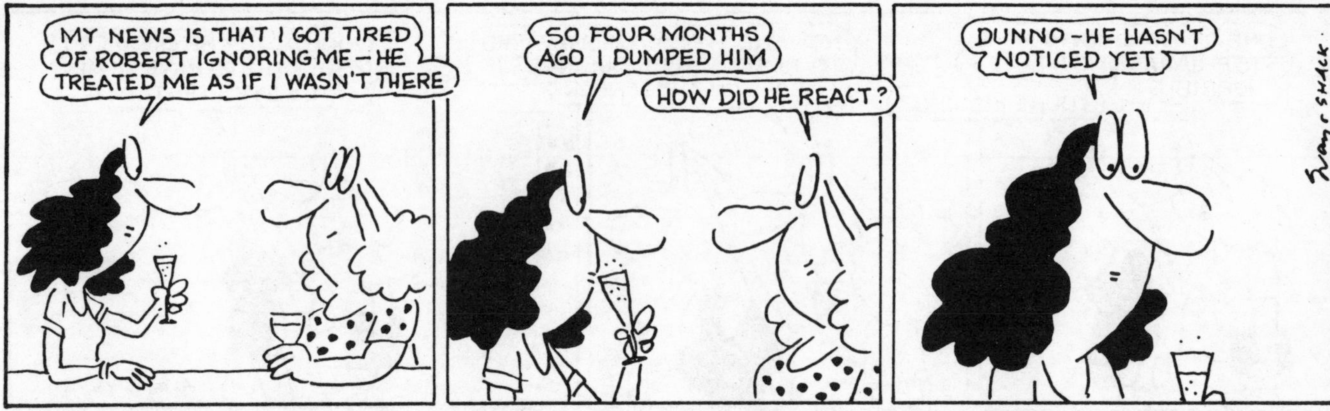
MY NEWS IS THAT I GOT TIRED OF ROBERT IGNORING ME – HE TREATED ME AS IF I WASN'T THERE
SO FOUR MONTHS AGO I DUMPED HIM
HOW DID HE REACT?
DUNNO – HE HASN'T NOTICED YET

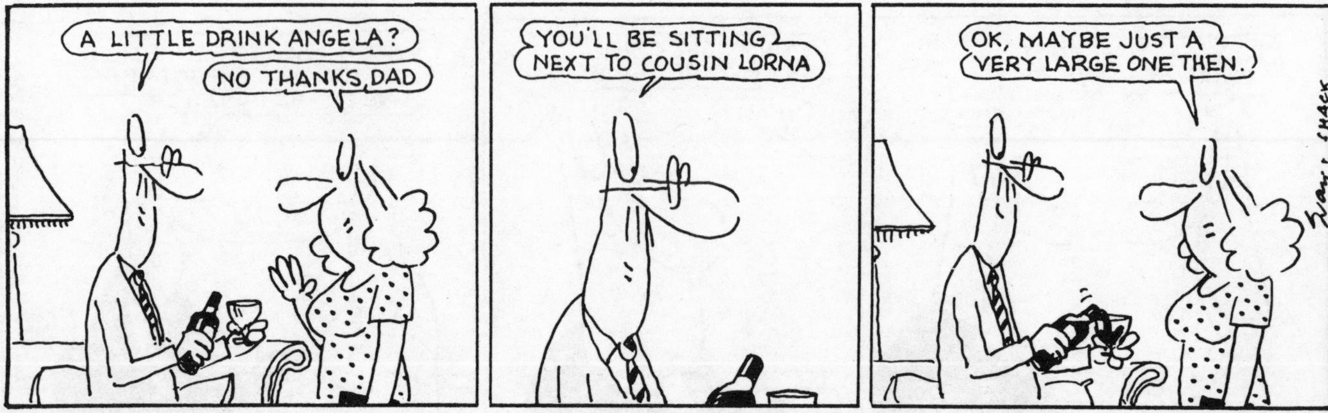
A LITTLE DRINK ANGELA?
NO THANKS, DAD
YOU'LL BE SITTING NEXT TO COUSIN LORNA
OK, MAYBE JUST A VERY LARGE ONE THEN.

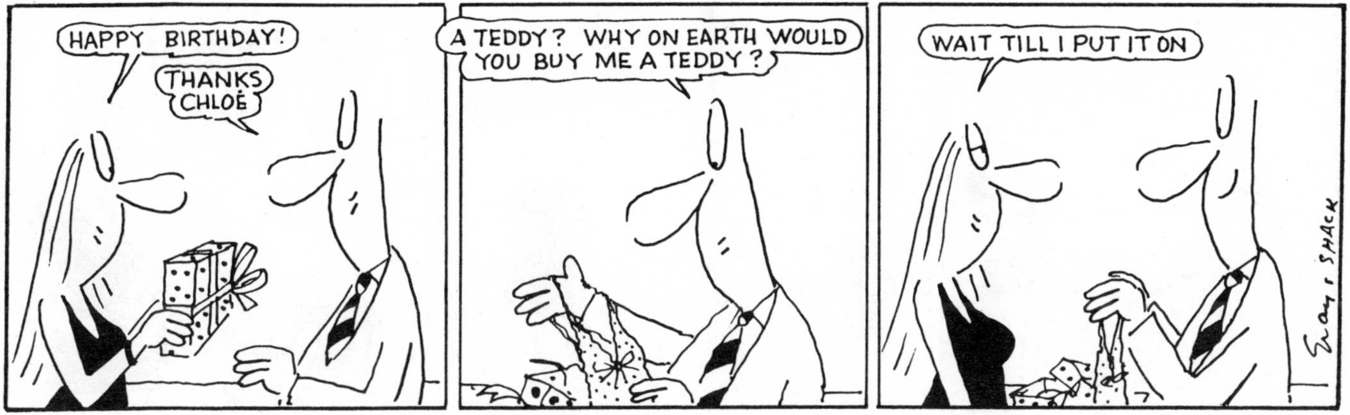
HAPPY BIRTHDAY!
THANKS CHLOË
A TEDDY? WHY ON EARTH WOULD YOU BUY ME A TEDDY?
WAIT TILL I PUT IT ON

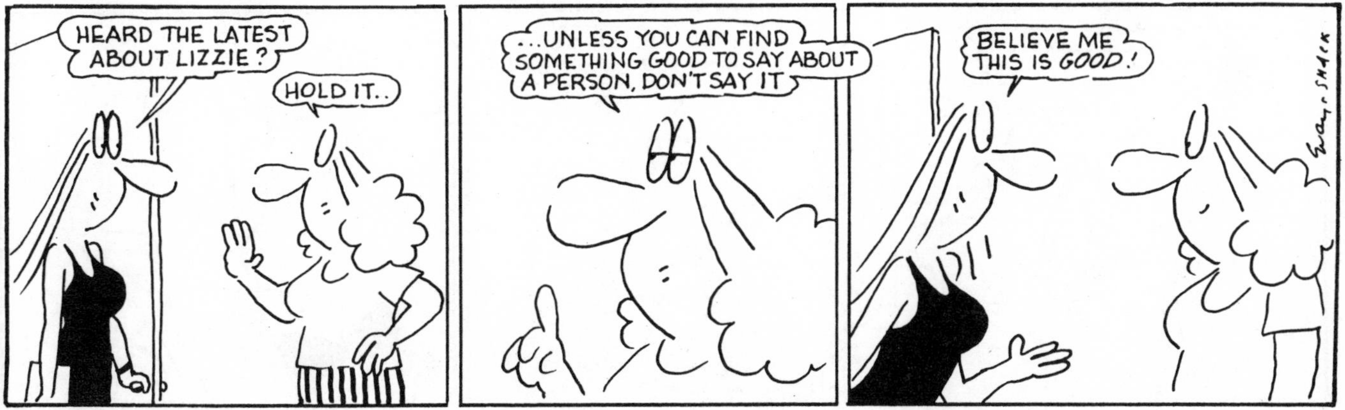
HEARD THE LATEST ABOUT LIZZIE?
HOLD IT..
...UNLESS YOU CAN FIND SOMETHING GOOD TO SAY ABOUT A PERSON, DON'T SAY IT
BELIEVE ME THIS IS *GOOD*!

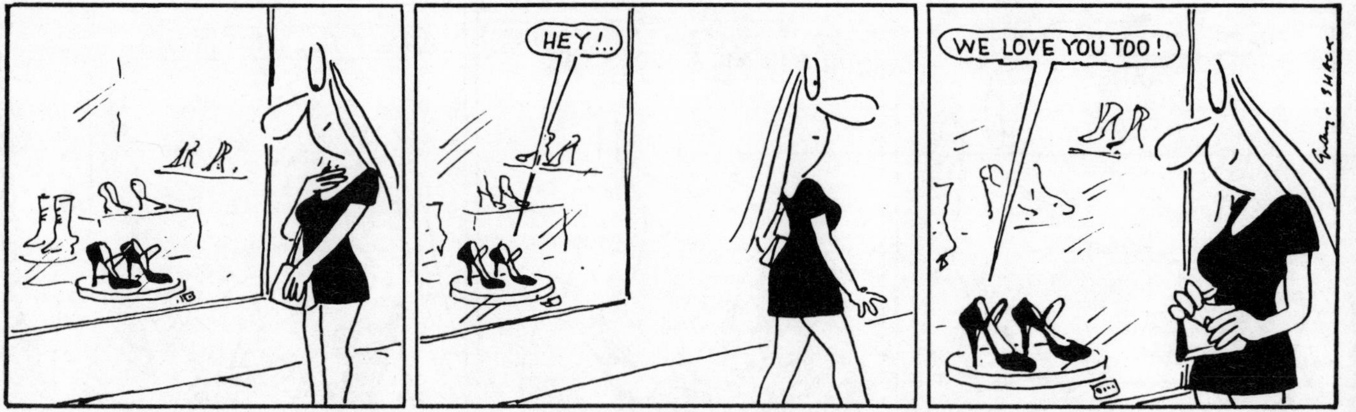
HEY!..
WE LOVE YOU TOO!

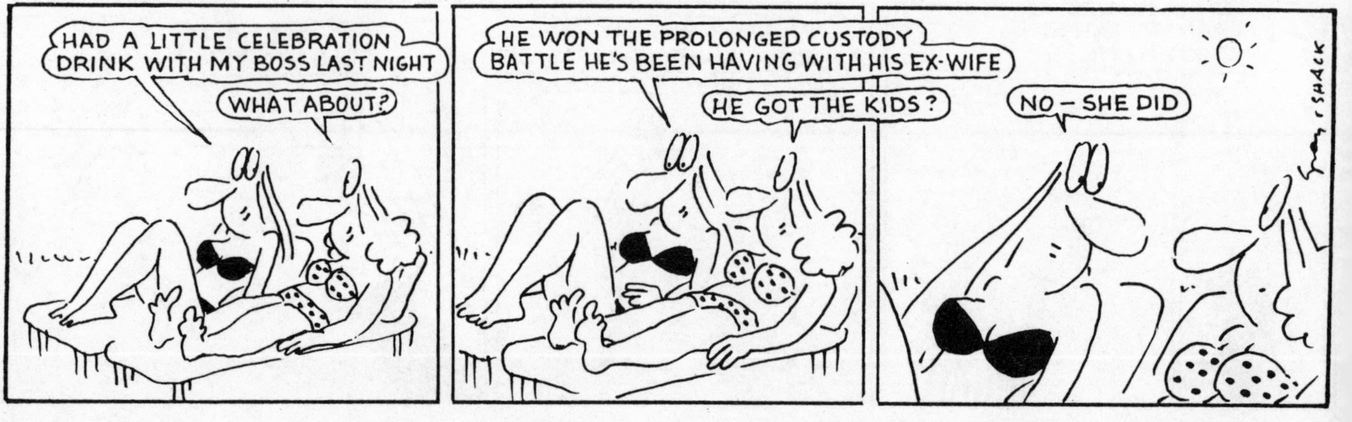
HAD A LITTLE CELEBRATION DRINK WITH MY BOSS LAST NIGHT
WHAT ABOUT?
HE WON THE PROLONGED CUSTODY BATTLE HE'S BEEN HAVING WITH HIS EX-WIFE
HE GOT THE KIDS?
NO – SHE DID

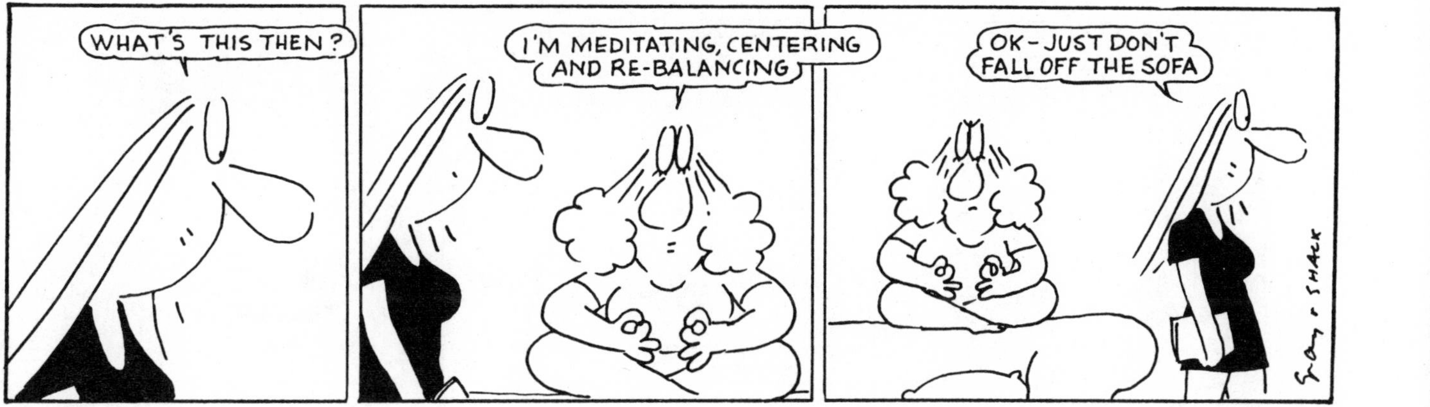
WHAT'S THIS THEN?
I'M MEDITATING, CENTERING AND RE-BALANCING
OK - JUST DON'T FALL OFF THE SOFA

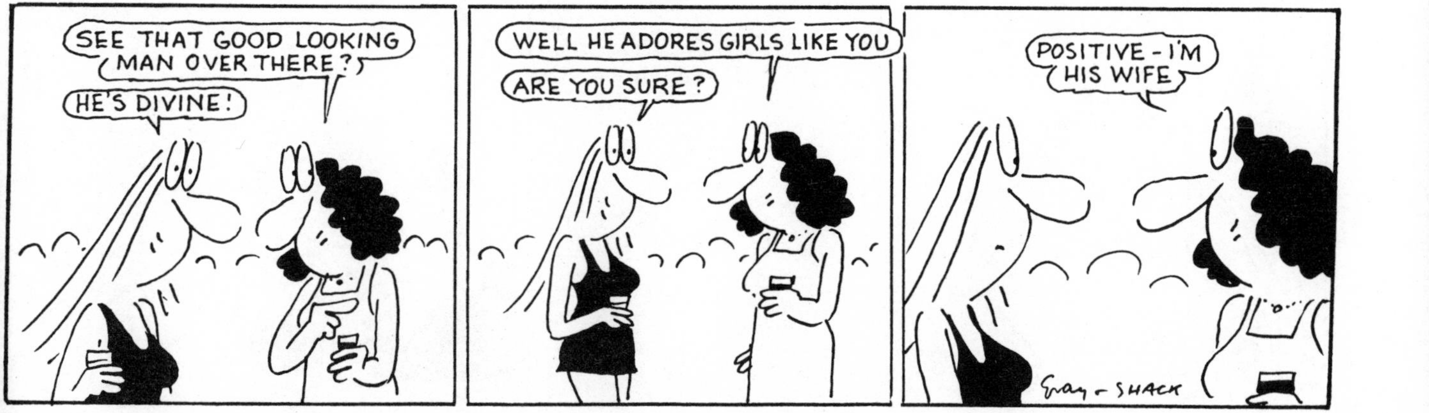
SEE THAT GOOD LOOKING MAN OVER THERE?
HE'S DIVINE!
WELL HE ADORES GIRLS LIKE YOU
ARE YOU SURE?
POSITIVE - I'M HIS WIFE

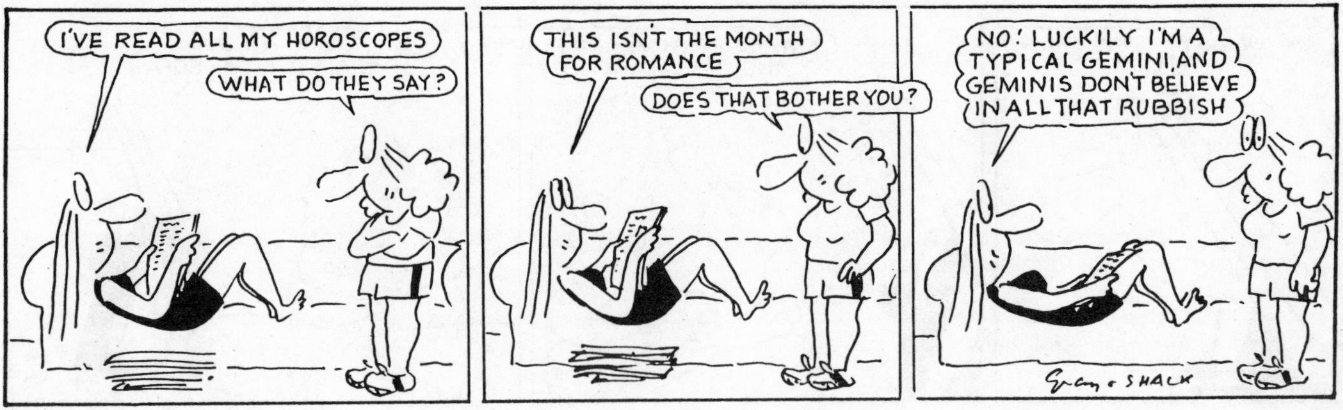
I'VE READ ALL MY HOROSCOPES
WHAT DO THEY SAY?
THIS ISN'T THE MONTH FOR ROMANCE
DOES THAT BOTHER YOU?
NO! LUCKILY I'M A TYPICAL GEMINI, AND GEMINIS DON'T BELIEVE IN ALL THAT RUBBISH

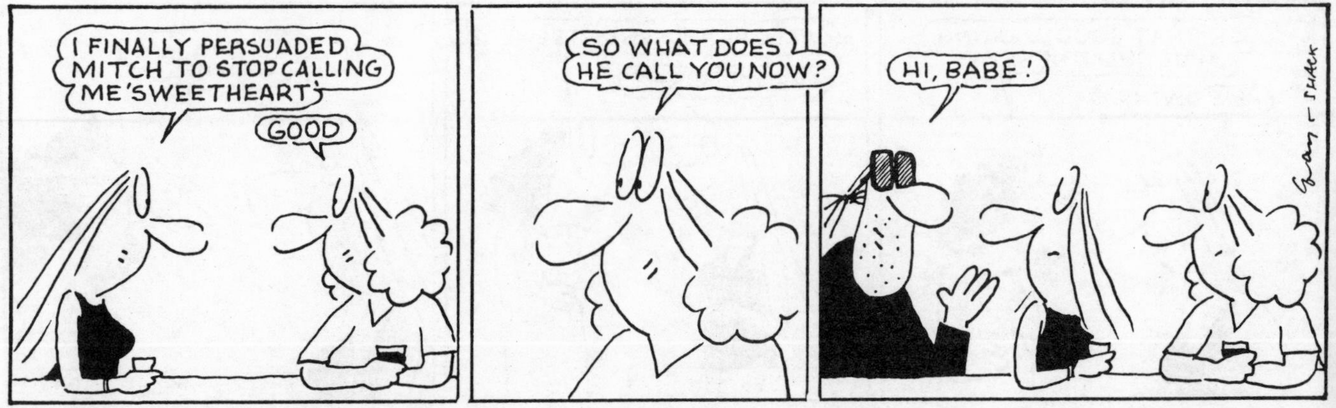
I FINALLY PERSUADED MITCH TO STOP CALLING ME 'SWEETHEART'
GOOD
SO WHAT DOES HE CALL YOU NOW?
HI, BABE!

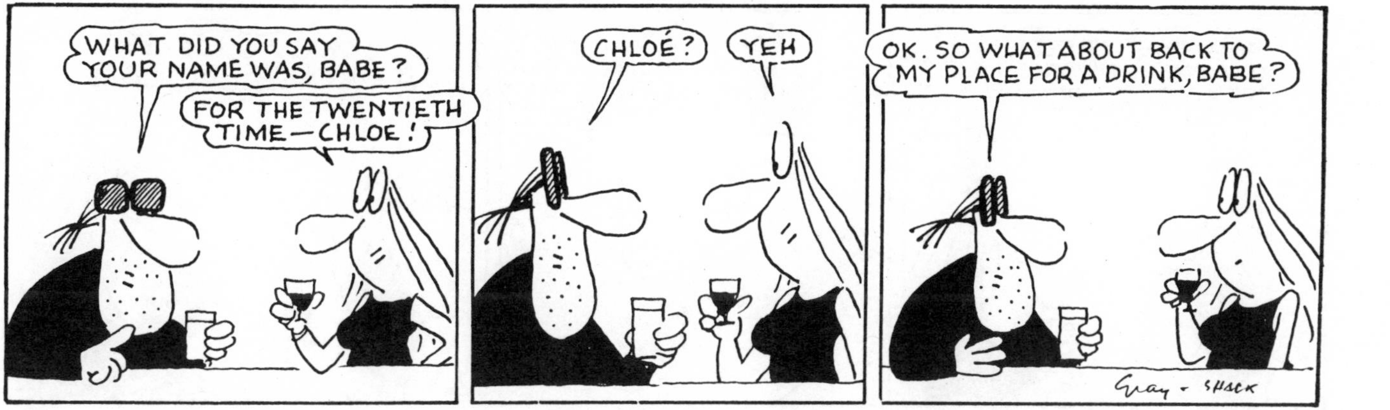
WHAT DID YOU SAY YOUR NAME WAS, BABE?
FOR THE TWENTIETH TIME—CHLOE!
CHLOÉ?
YEH
OK. SO WHAT ABOUT BACK TO MY PLACE FOR A DRINK, BABE?
Gray • SHACK

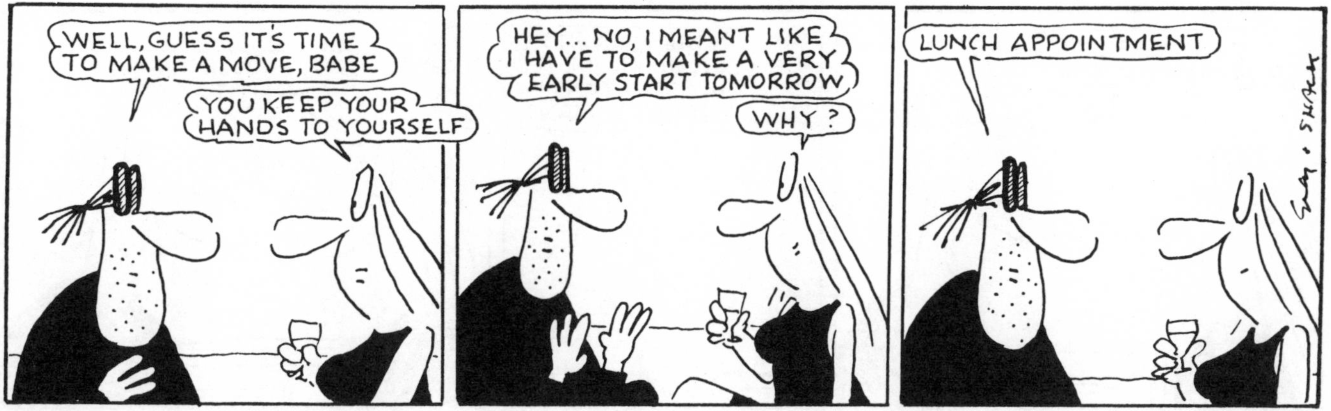
WELL, GUESS IT'S TIME TO MAKE A MOVE, BABE
YOU KEEP YOUR HANDS TO YOURSELF
HEY... NO, I MEANT LIKE I HAVE TO MAKE A VERY EARLY START TOMORROW
WHY?
LUNCH APPOINTMENT
Gray • SHACK

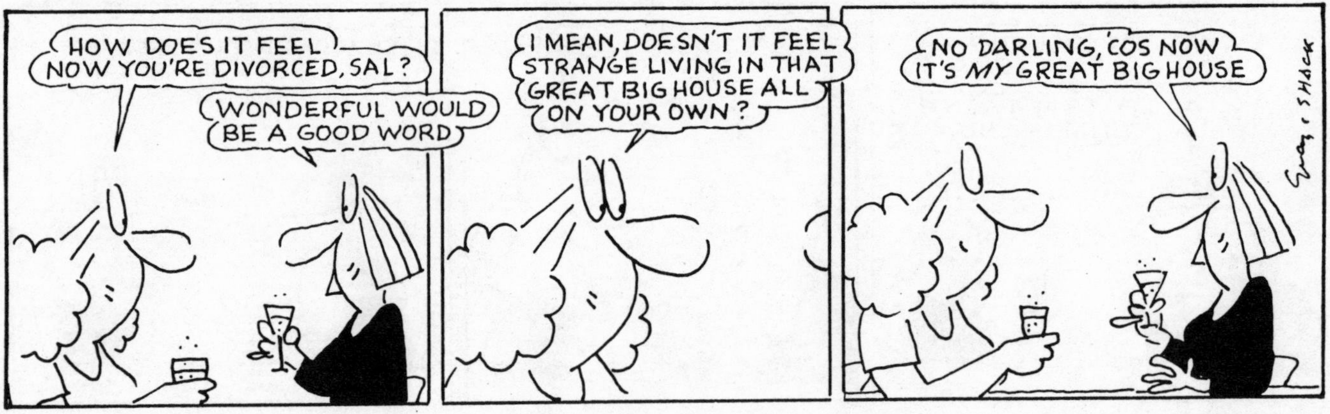
HOW DOES IT FEEL NOW YOU'RE DIVORCED, SAL?
WONDERFUL WOULD BE A GOOD WORD
I MEAN, DOESN'T IT FEEL STRANGE LIVING IN THAT GREAT BIG HOUSE ALL ON YOUR OWN?
NO DARLING, 'COS NOW IT'S *MY* GREAT BIG HOUSE

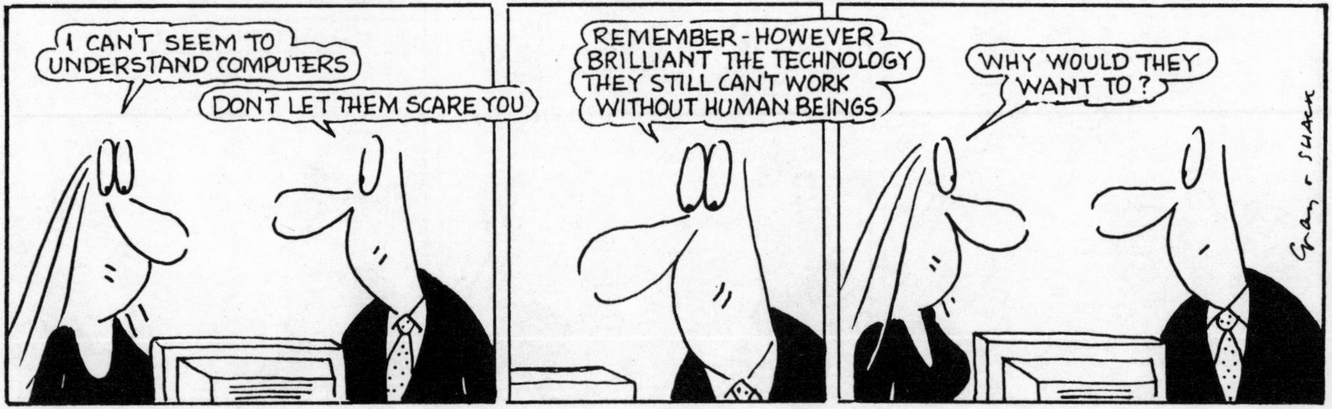
I CAN'T SEEM TO UNDERSTAND COMPUTERS
DON'T LET THEM SCARE YOU
REMEMBER - HOWEVER BRILLIANT THE TECHNOLOGY THEY STILL CAN'T WORK WITHOUT HUMAN BEINGS
WHY WOULD THEY WANT TO?

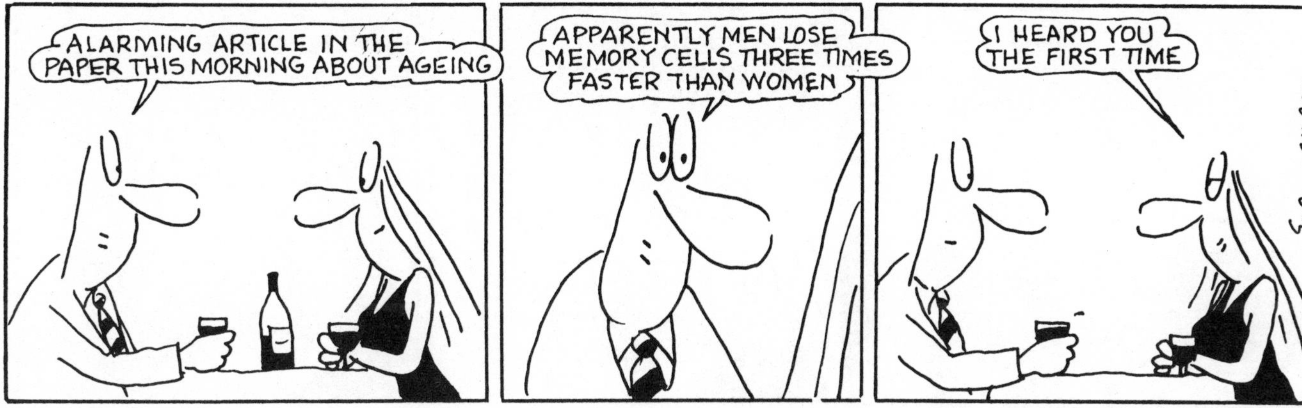
ALARMING ARTICLE IN THE PAPER THIS MORNING ABOUT AGEING
APPARENTLY MEN LOSE MEMORY CELLS THREE TIMES FASTER THAN WOMEN
I HEARD YOU THE FIRST TIME

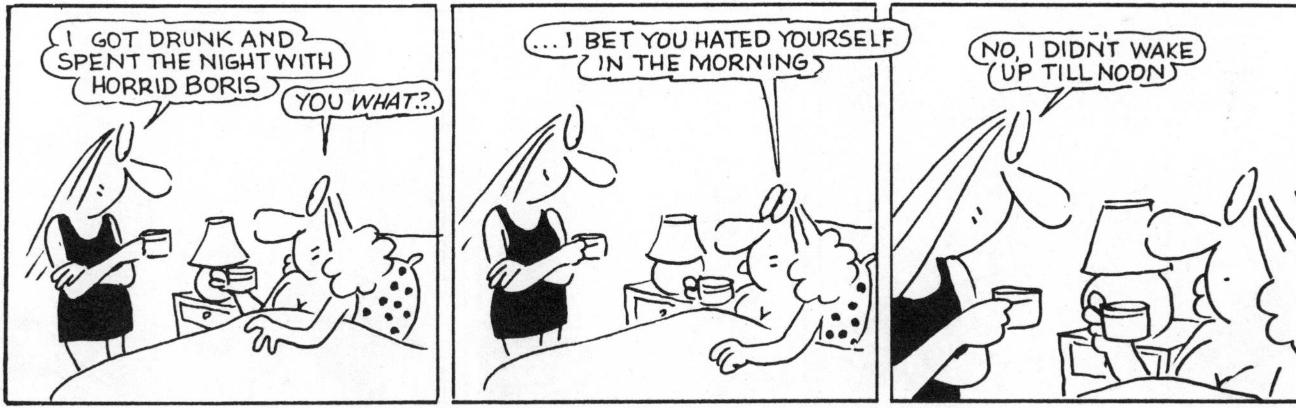
I GOT DRUNK AND SPENT THE NIGHT WITH HORRID BORIS
YOU WHAT?.
... I BET YOU HATED YOURSELF IN THE MORNING
NO, I DIDN'T WAKE UP TILL NOON

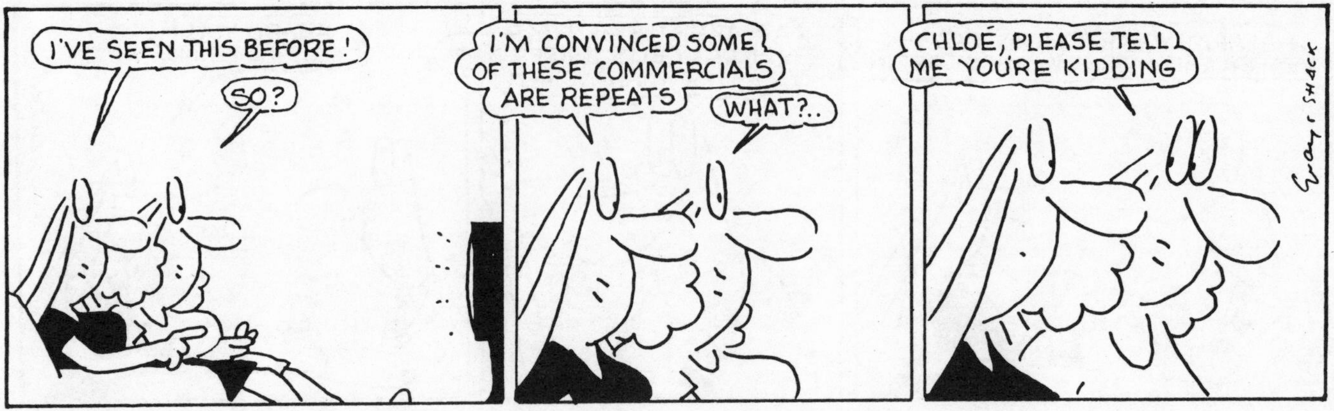
I'VE SEEN THIS BEFORE!
SO?
I'M CONVINCED SOME OF THESE COMMERCIALS ARE REPEATS
WHAT?..
CHLOÉ, PLEASE TELL ME YOU'RE KIDDING

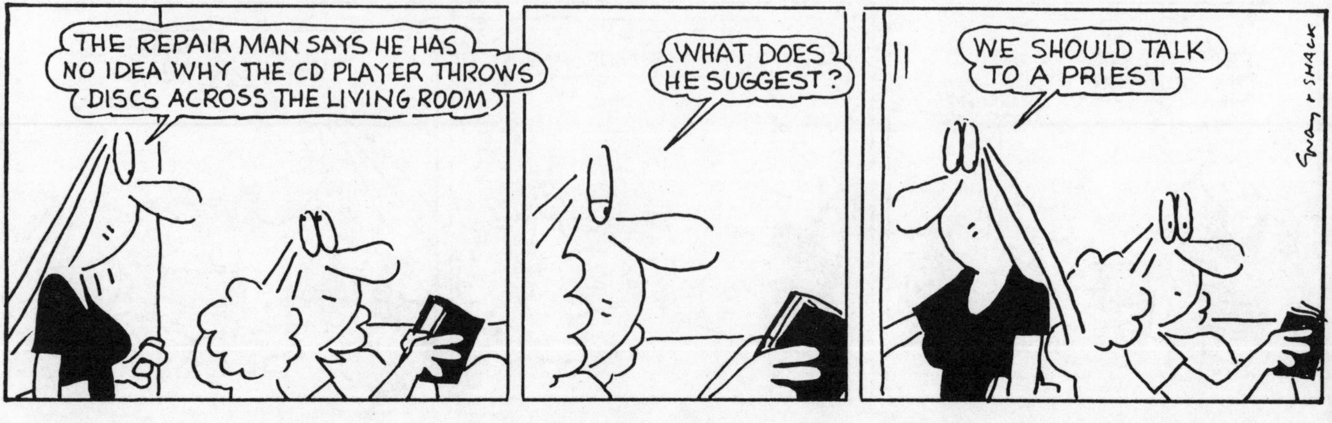
THE REPAIR MAN SAYS HE HAS NO IDEA WHY THE CD PLAYER THROWS DISCS ACROSS THE LIVING ROOM
WHAT DOES HE SUGGEST?
WE SHOULD TALK TO A PRIEST

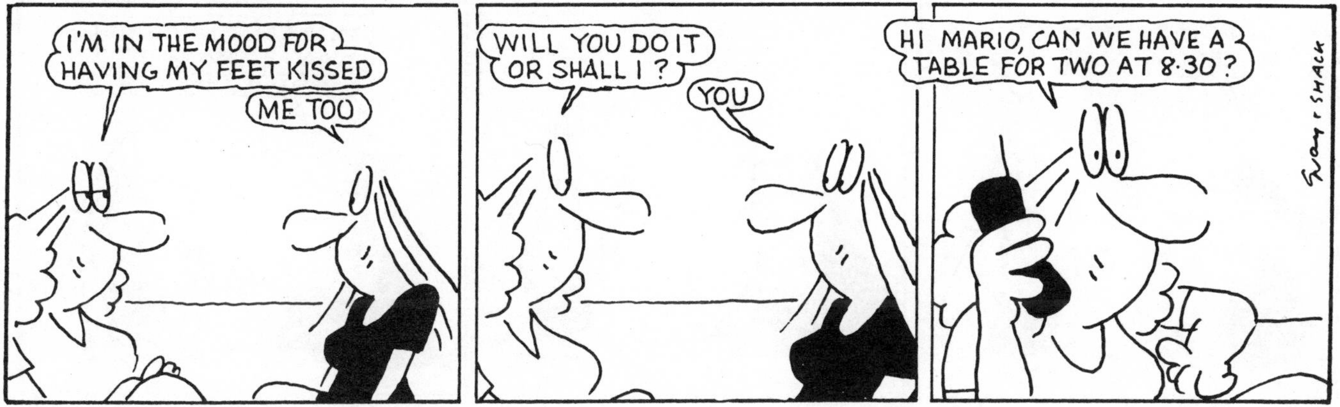
I'M IN THE MOOD FOR HAVING MY FEET KISSED
ME TOO
WILL YOU DO IT OR SHALL I ?
YOU
HI MARIO, CAN WE HAVE A TABLE FOR TWO AT 8·30 ?

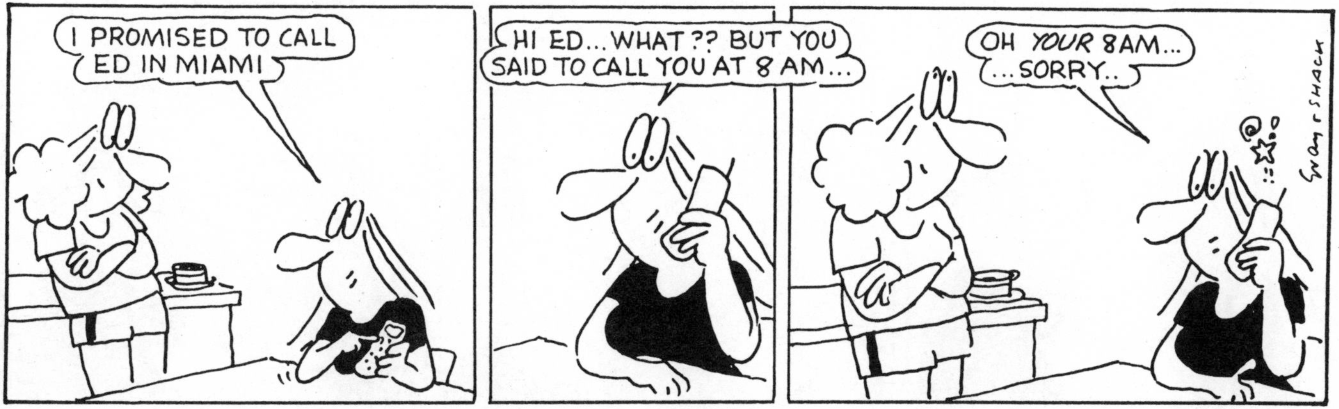
I PROMISED TO CALL ED IN MIAMI
HI ED... WHAT ?? BUT YOU SAID TO CALL YOU AT 8 AM...
OH *YOUR* 8AM... ...SORRY..

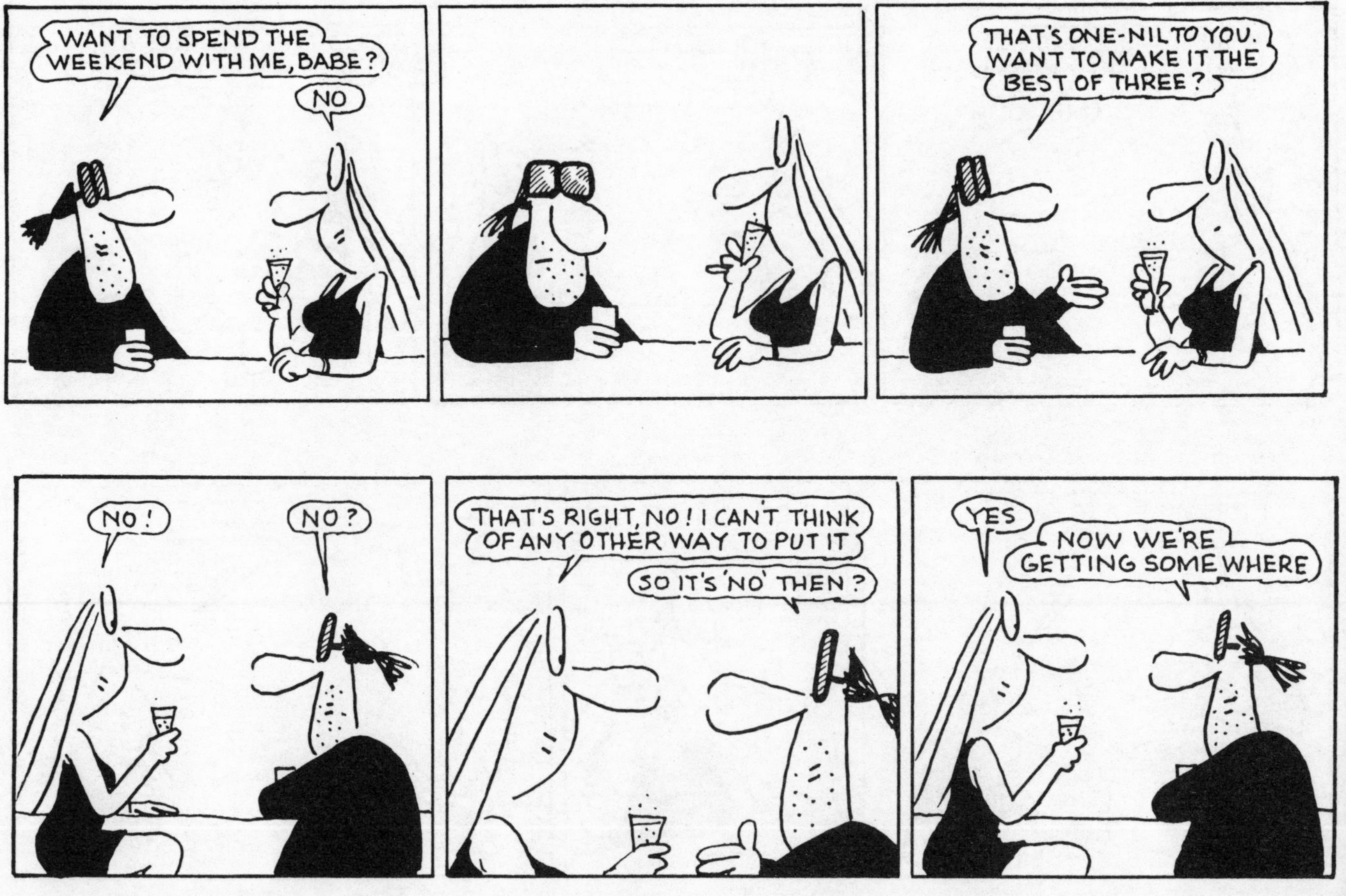
WANT TO SPEND THE WEEKEND WITH ME, BABE?
NO
THAT'S ONE-NIL TO YOU. WANT TO MAKE IT THE BEST OF THREE?
NO!
NO?
THAT'S RIGHT, NO! I CAN'T THINK OF ANY OTHER WAY TO PUT IT
SO IT'S 'NO' THEN?
YES
NOW WE'RE GETTING SOMEWHERE

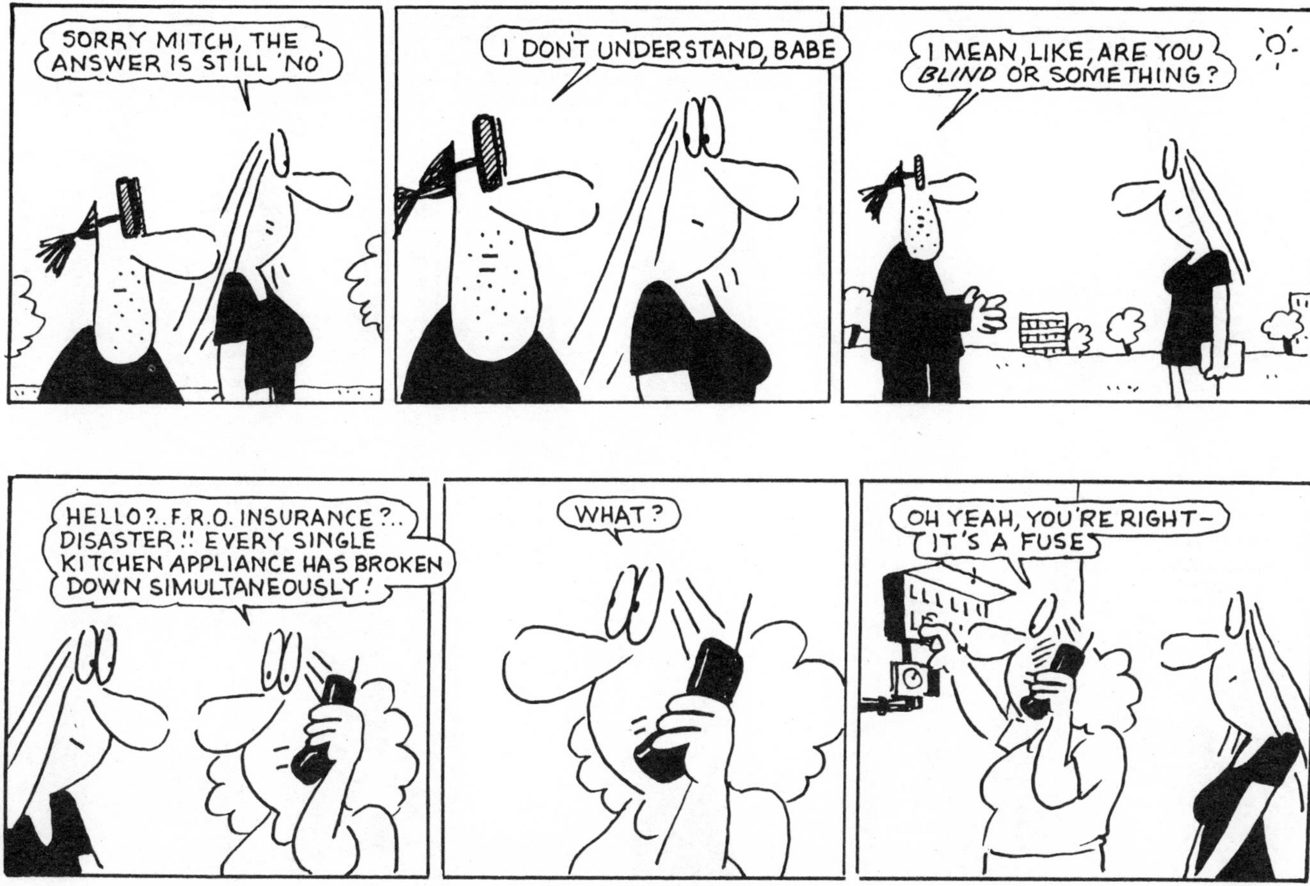
SORRY MITCH, THE ANSWER IS STILL 'NO'
I DON'T UNDERSTAND, BABE
I MEAN, LIKE, ARE YOU *BLIND* OR SOMETHING?
HELLO?.. F.R.O. INSURANCE?.. DISASTER!! EVERY SINGLE KITCHEN APPLIANCE HAS BROKEN DOWN SIMULTANEOUSLY!
WHAT?
OH YEAH, YOU'RE RIGHT– IT'S A FUSE

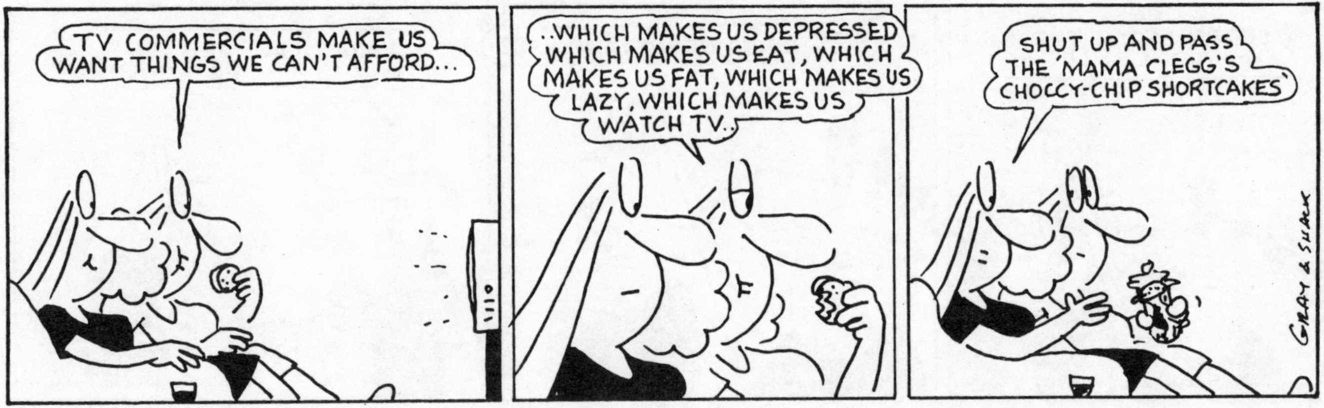
TV COMMERCIALS MAKE US WANT THINGS WE CAN'T AFFORD...
..WHICH MAKES US DEPRESSED WHICH MAKES US EAT, WHICH MAKES US FAT, WHICH MAKES US LAZY, WHICH MAKES US WATCH TV..
SHUT UP AND PASS THE 'MAMA CLEGG'S CHOCCY-CHIP SHORTCAKES'
GRAY & SHACK

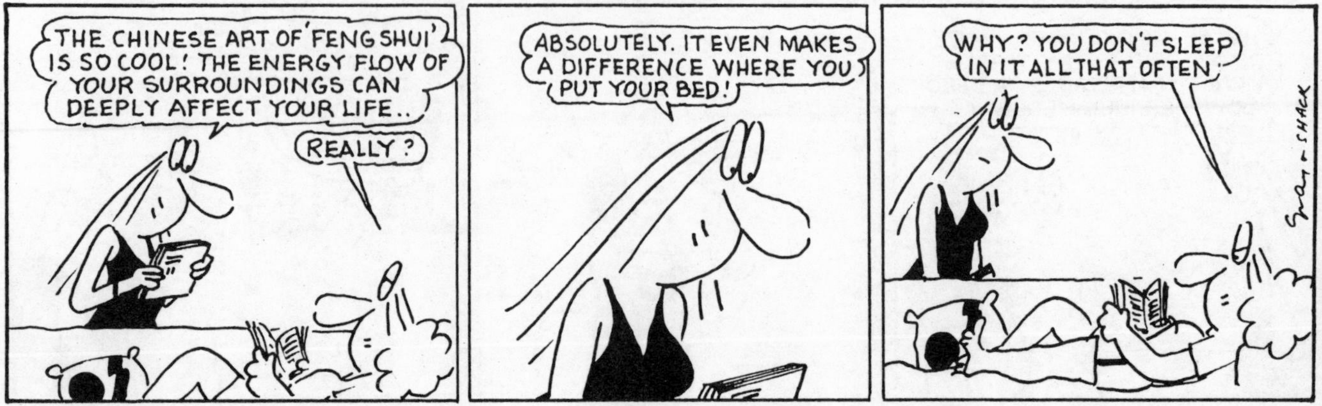
THE CHINESE ART OF 'FENG SHUI' IS SO COOL! THE ENERGY FLOW OF YOUR SURROUNDINGS CAN DEEPLY AFFECT YOUR LIFE..
REALLY?
ABSOLUTELY. IT EVEN MAKES A DIFFERENCE WHERE YOU PUT YOUR BED!
WHY? YOU DON'T SLEEP IN IT ALL THAT OFTEN
Gray - SHACK

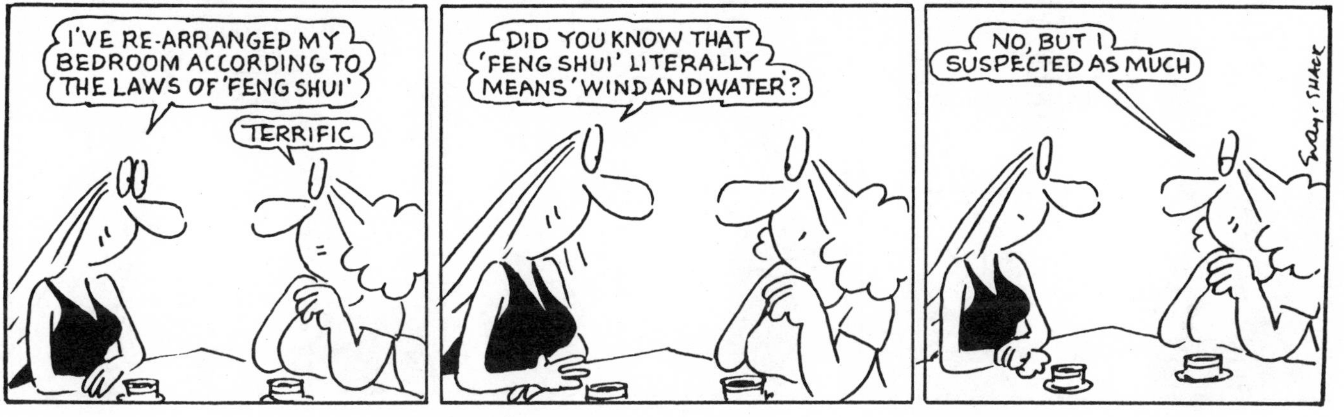
I'VE RE-ARRANGED MY BEDROOM ACCORDING TO THE LAWS OF 'FENG SHUI'
TERRIFIC
DID YOU KNOW THAT 'FENG SHUI' LITERALLY MEANS 'WIND AND WATER'?
NO, BUT I SUSPECTED AS MUCH

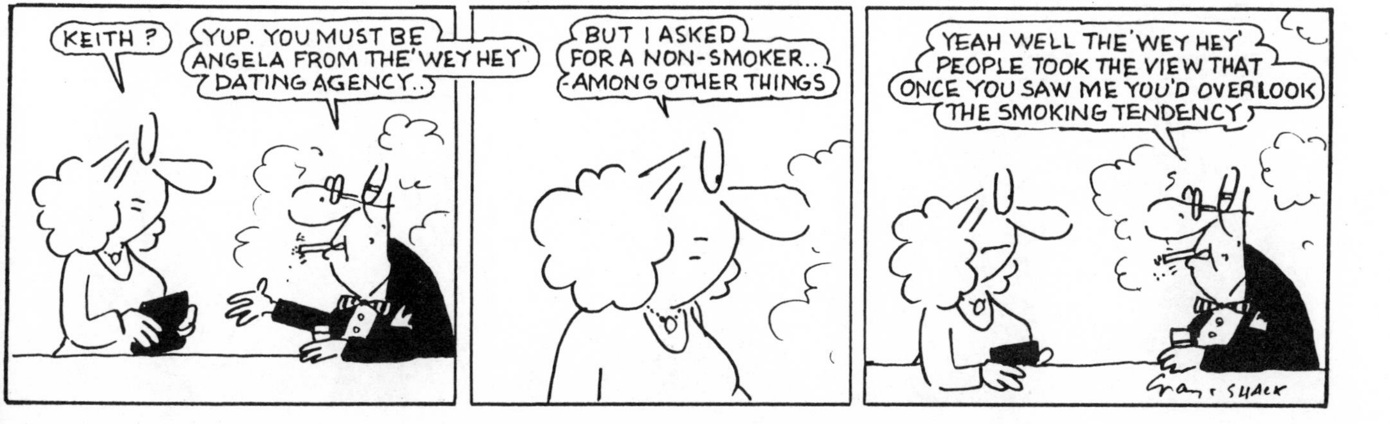
KEITH ?
YUP. YOU MUST BE ANGELA FROM THE 'WEY HEY' DATING AGENCY..
BUT I ASKED FOR A NON-SMOKER.. -AMONG OTHER THINGS
YEAH WELL THE 'WEY HEY' PEOPLE TOOK THE VIEW THAT ONCE YOU SAW ME YOU'D OVERLOOK THE SMOKING TENDENCY
Gray + SHACK

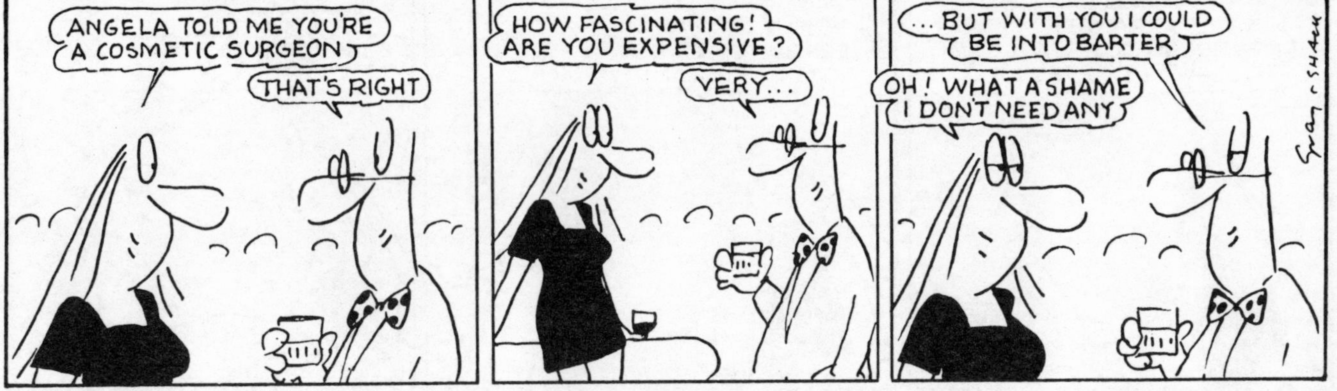
ANGELA TOLD ME YOU'RE A COSMETIC SURGEON
THAT'S RIGHT
HOW FASCINATING! ARE YOU EXPENSIVE?
VERY...
OH! WHAT A SHAME I DON'T NEED ANY
... BUT WITH YOU I COULD BE INTO BARTER

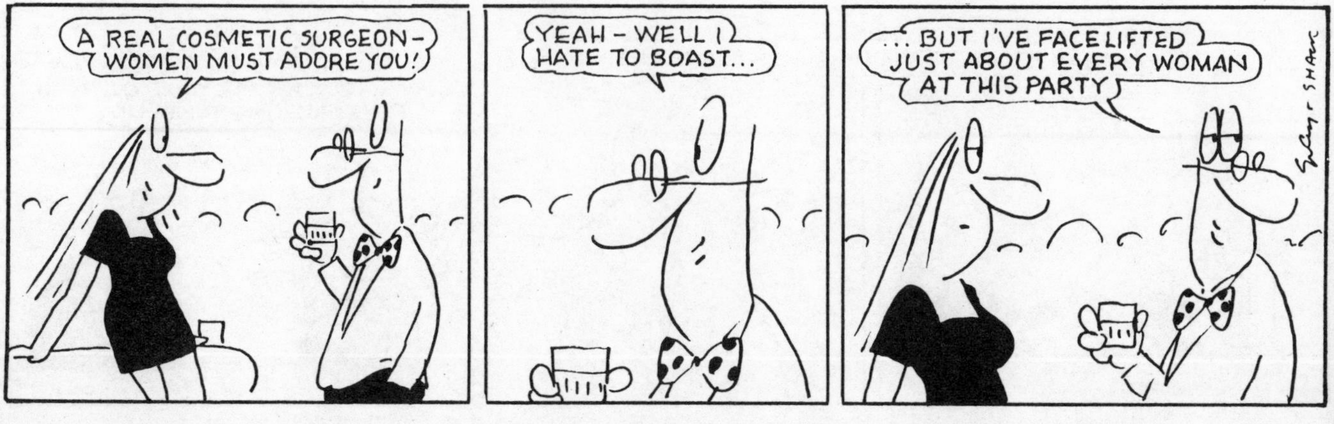
A REAL COSMETIC SURGEON – WOMEN MUST ADORE YOU!
YEAH – WELL I HATE TO BOAST...
... BUT I'VE FACE LIFTED JUST ABOUT EVERY WOMAN AT THIS PARTY

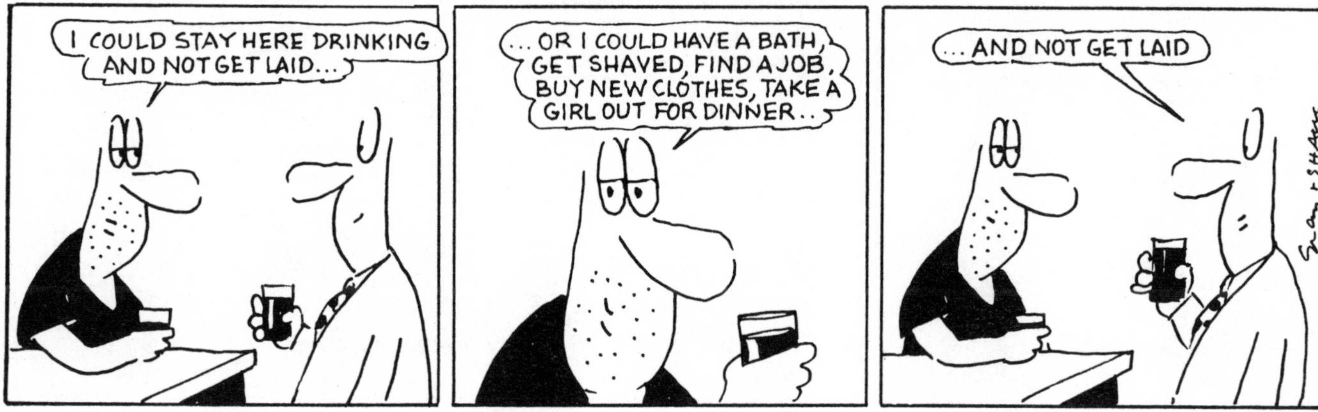
I COULD STAY HERE DRINKING AND NOT GET LAID...
... OR I COULD HAVE A BATH, GET SHAVED, FIND A JOB, BUY NEW CLOTHES, TAKE A GIRL OUT FOR DINNER..
... AND NOT GET LAID

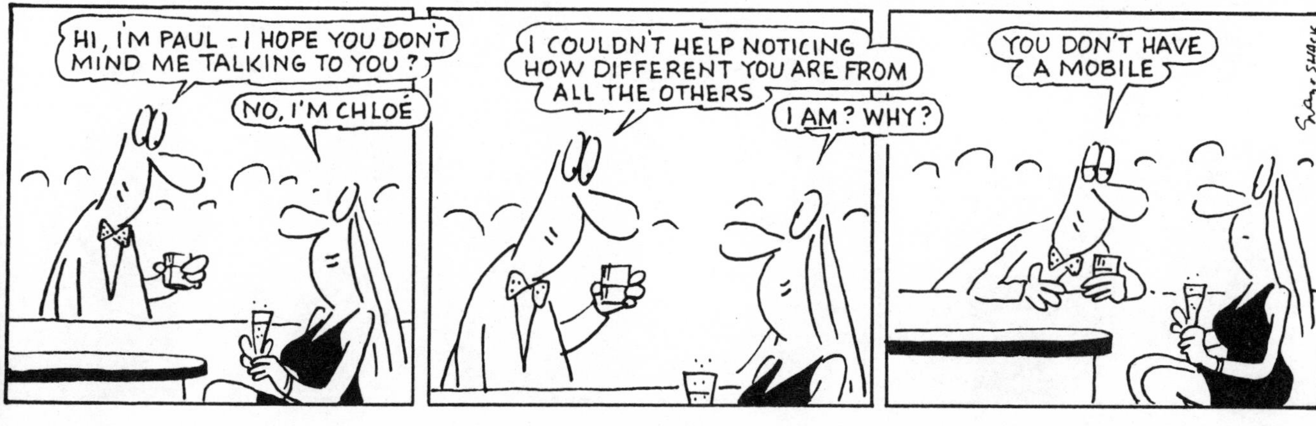
HI, I'M PAUL - I HOPE YOU DON'T MIND ME TALKING TO YOU?
NO, I'M CHLOÉ
I COULDN'T HELP NOTICING HOW DIFFERENT YOU ARE FROM ALL THE OTHERS
I AM? WHY?
YOU DON'T HAVE A MOBILE

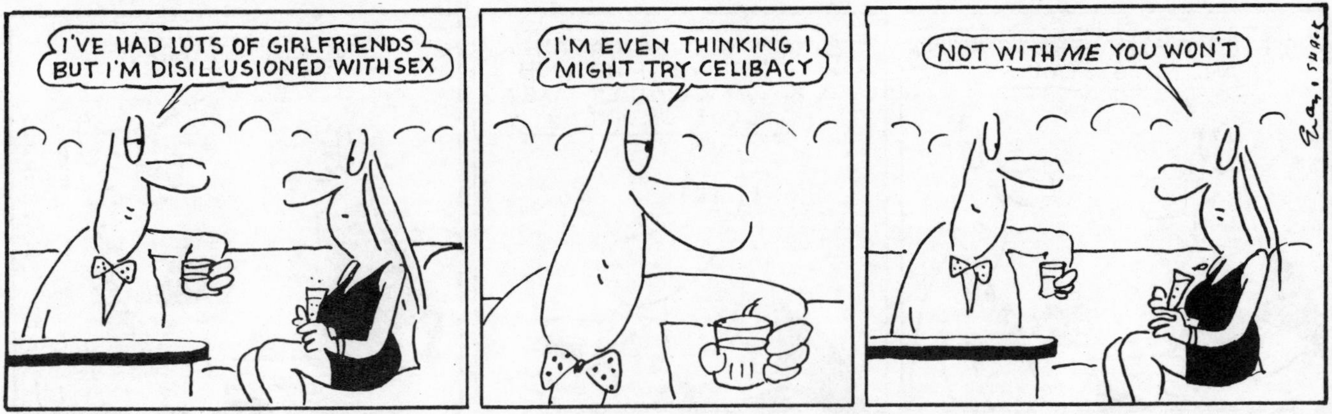
I'VE HAD LOTS OF GIRLFRIENDS BUT I'M DISILLUSIONED WITH SEX
I'M EVEN THINKING I MIGHT TRY CELIBACY
NOT WITH *ME* YOU WON'T

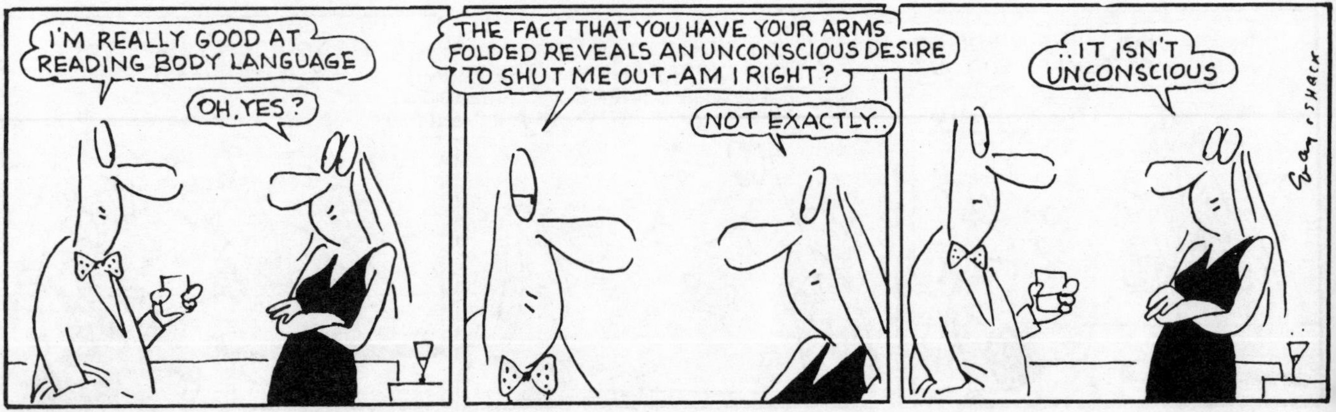
I'M REALLY GOOD AT READING BODY LANGUAGE
OH, YES?
THE FACT THAT YOU HAVE YOUR ARMS FOLDED REVEALS AN UNCONSCIOUS DESIRE TO SHUT ME OUT-AM I RIGHT?
NOT EXACTLY..
..IT ISN'T UNCONSCIOUS

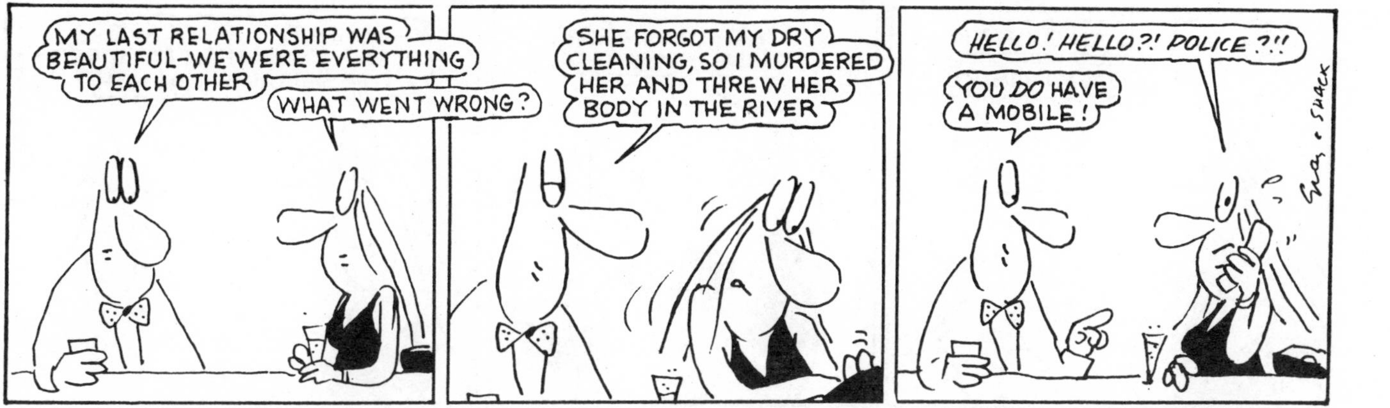
MY LAST RELATIONSHIP WAS BEAUTIFUL-WE WERE EVERYTHING TO EACH OTHER
WHAT WENT WRONG?
SHE FORGOT MY DRY CLEANING, SO I MURDERED HER AND THREW HER BODY IN THE RIVER
HELLO! HELLO?! POLICE?!!
YOU *DO* HAVE A MOBILE!

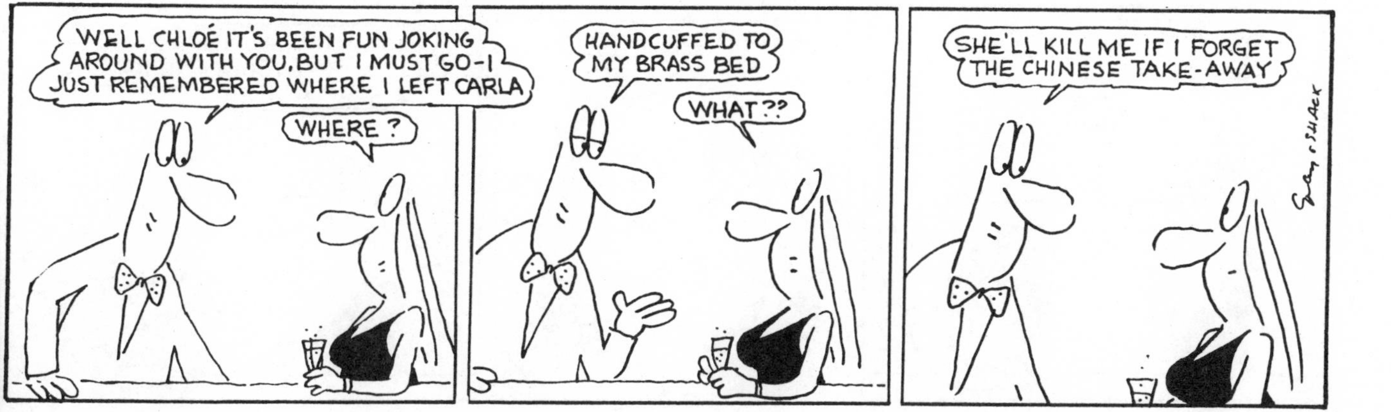
WELL CHLOÉ IT'S BEEN FUN JOKING AROUND WITH YOU, BUT I MUST GO-I JUST REMEMBERED WHERE I LEFT CARLA
WHERE?
HANDCUFFED TO MY BRASS BED
WHAT??
SHE'LL KILL ME IF I FORGET THE CHINESE TAKE-AWAY

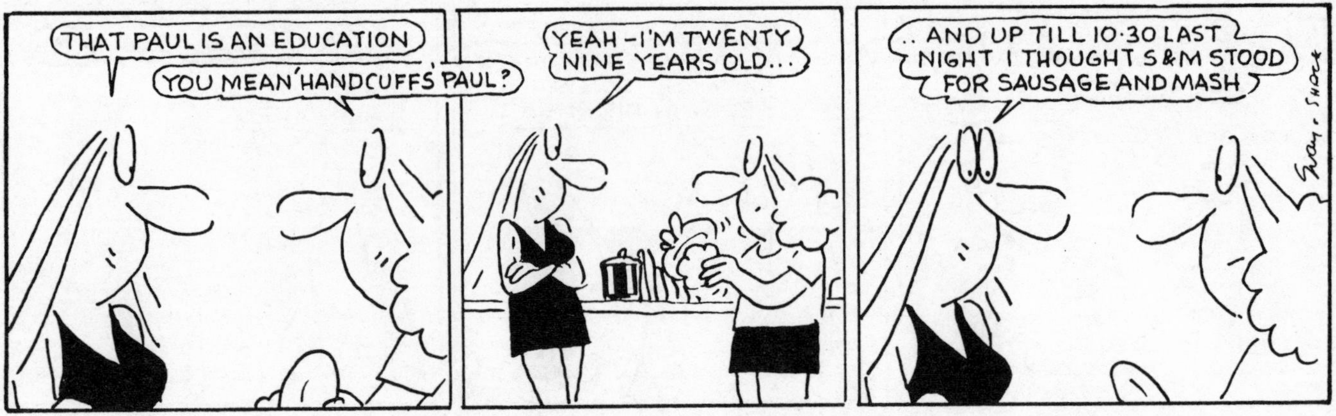
THAT PAUL IS AN EDUCATION
YOU MEAN 'HANDCUFFS' PAUL?
YEAH – I'M TWENTY NINE YEARS OLD...
.. AND UP TILL 10·30 LAST NIGHT I THOUGHT S&M STOOD FOR SAUSAGE AND MASH

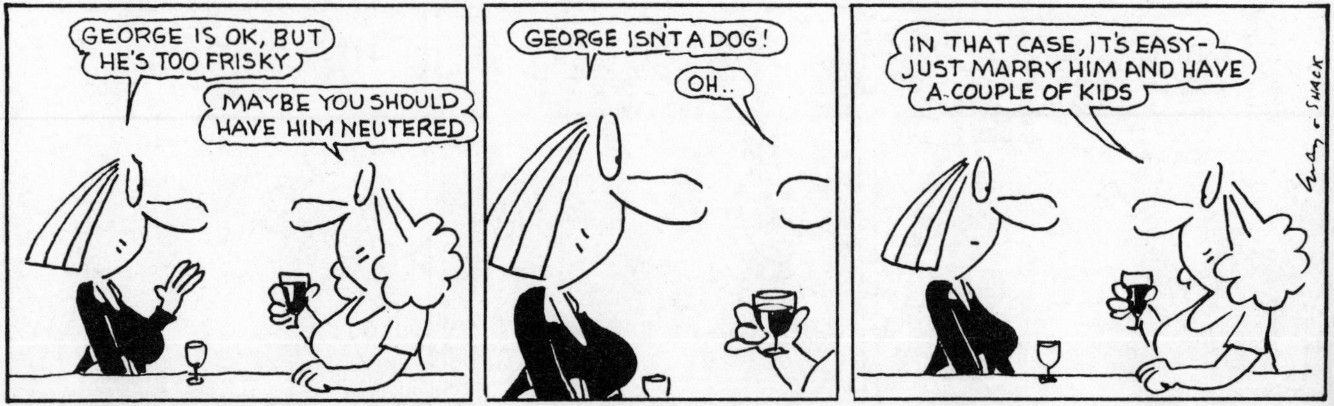
GEORGE IS OK, BUT HE'S TOO FRISKY
MAYBE YOU SHOULD HAVE HIM NEUTERED
GEORGE ISN'T A DOG!
OH..
IN THAT CASE, IT'S EASY – JUST MARRY HIM AND HAVE A COUPLE OF KIDS

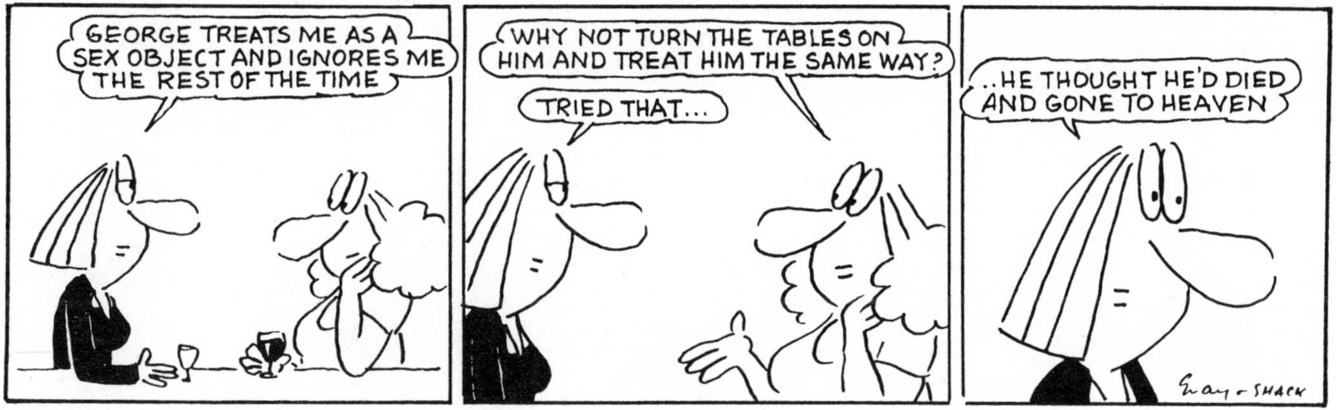

GEORGE TREATS ME AS A SEX OBJECT AND IGNORES ME THE REST OF THE TIME
WHY NOT TURN THE TABLES ON HIM AND TREAT HIM THE SAME WAY?
TRIED THAT...
..HE THOUGHT HE'D DIED AND GONE TO HEAVEN

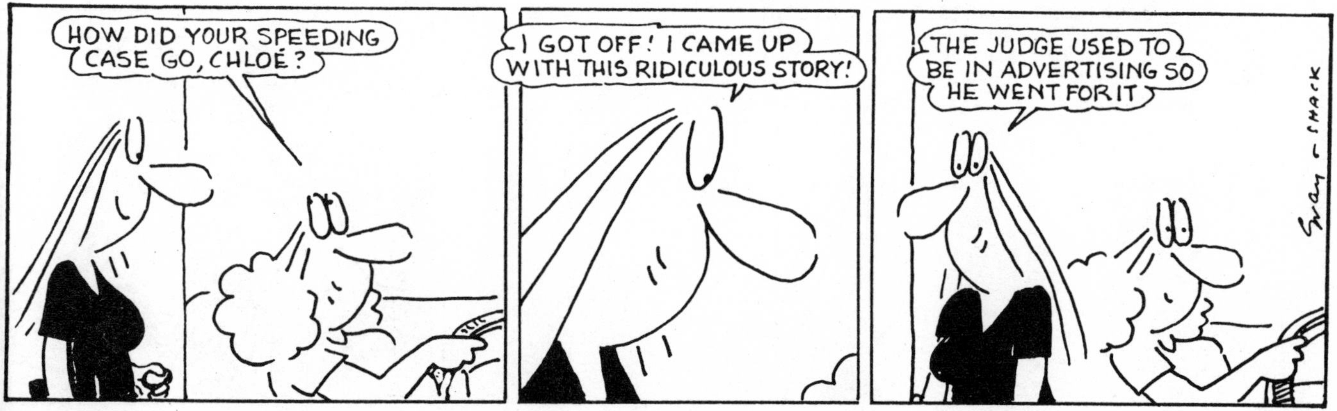

HOW DID YOUR SPEEDING CASE GO, CHLOÉ?
I GOT OFF! I CAME UP WITH THIS RIDICULOUS STORY!
THE JUDGE USED TO BE IN ADVERTISING SO HE WENT FOR IT

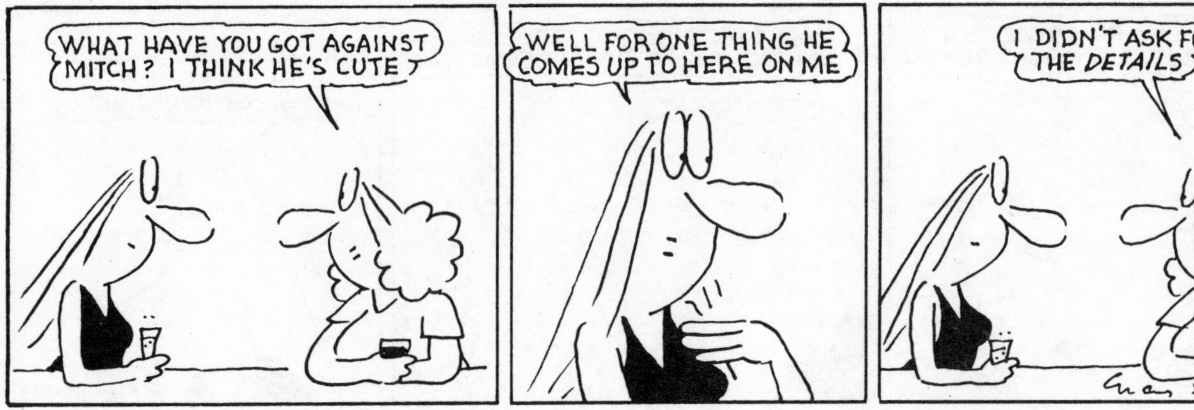
WHAT HAVE YOU GOT AGAINST MITCH? I THINK HE'S CUTE
WELL FOR ONE THING HE COMES UP TO HERE ON ME
I DIDN'T ASK FOR THE *DETAILS*
& SHACK

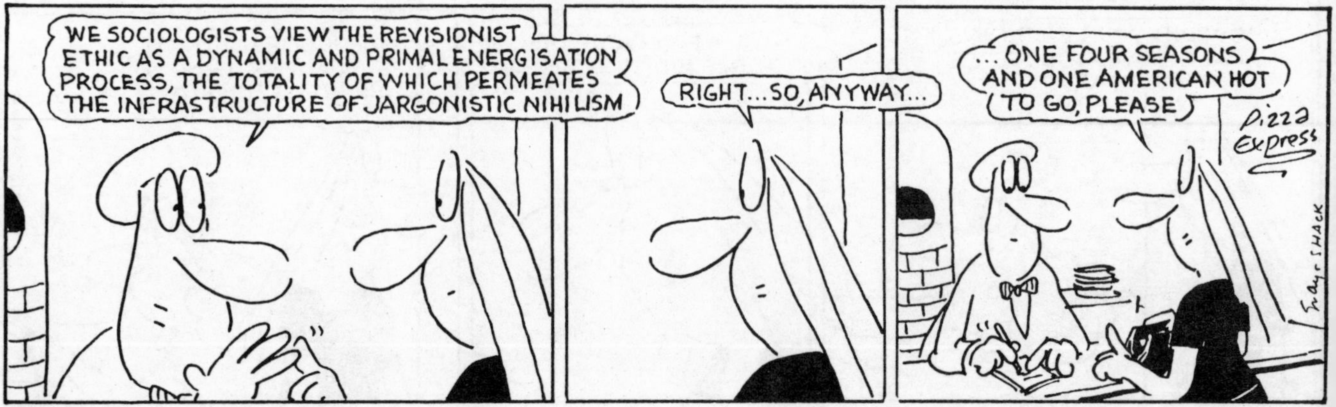
WE SOCIOLOGISTS VIEW THE REVISIONIST ETHIC AS A DYNAMIC AND PRIMAL ENERGISATION PROCESS, THE TOTALITY OF WHICH PERMEATES THE INFRASTRUCTURE OF JARGONISTIC NIHILISM
RIGHT... SO, ANYWAY...
... ONE FOUR SEASONS AND ONE AMERICAN HOT TO GO, PLEASE
Pizza Express
SHACK

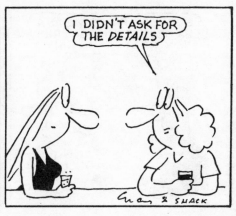

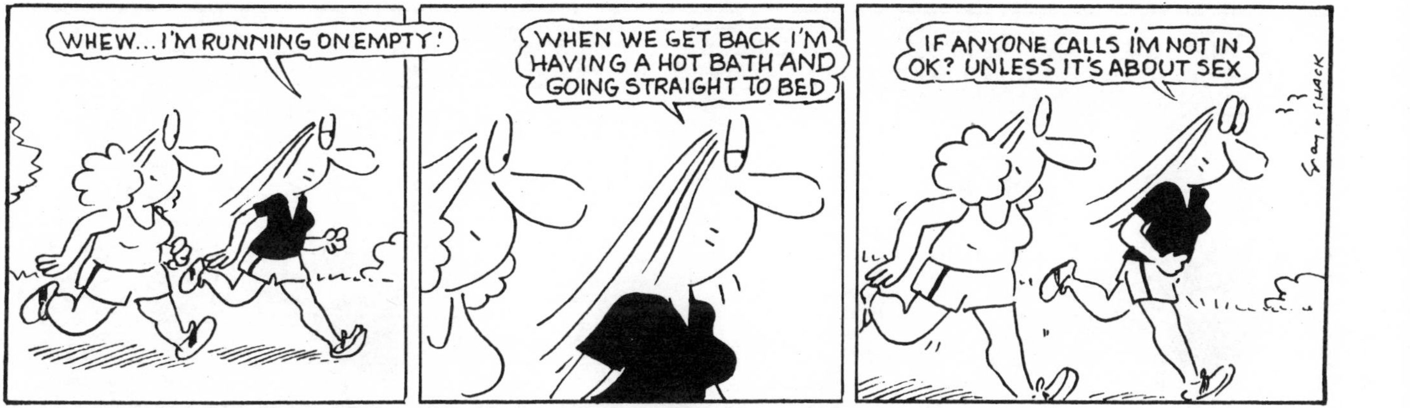
WHEW... I'M RUNNING ON EMPTY!
WHEN WE GET BACK I'M HAVING A HOT BATH AND GOING STRAIGHT TO BED
IF ANYONE CALLS I'M NOT IN OK? UNLESS IT'S ABOUT SEX

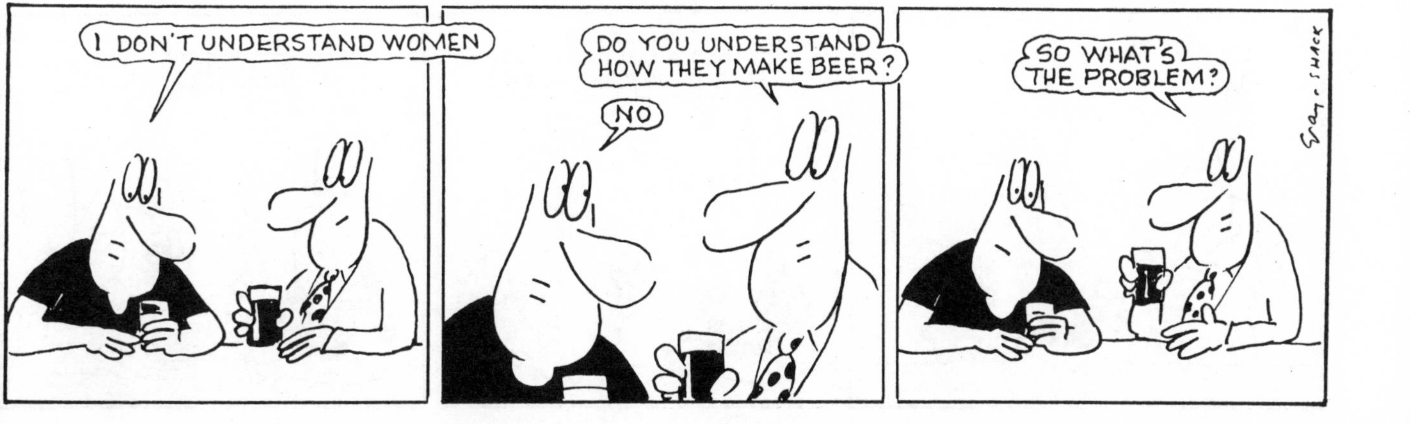
I DON'T UNDERSTAND WOMEN
DO YOU UNDERSTAND HOW THEY MAKE BEER?
NO
SO WHAT'S THE PROBLEM?

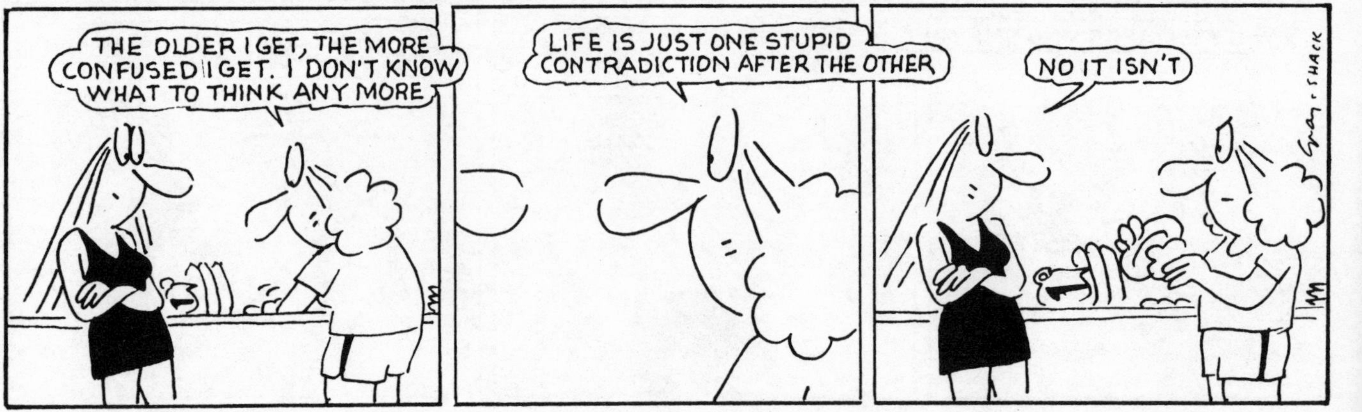
THE OLDER I GET, THE MORE CONFUSED I GET. I DON'T KNOW WHAT TO THINK ANY MORE
LIFE IS JUST ONE STUPID CONTRADICTION AFTER THE OTHER
NO IT ISN'T

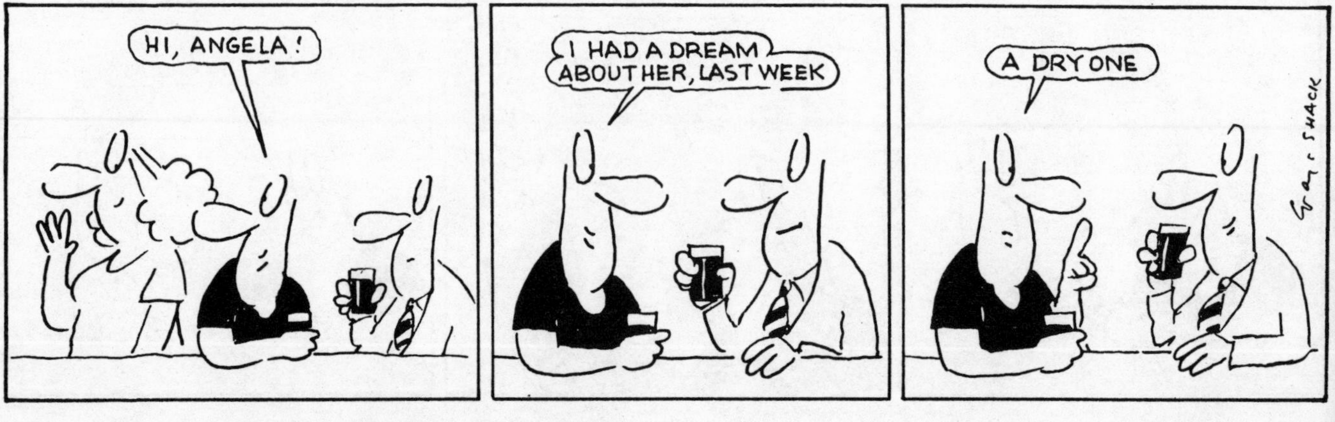
HI, ANGELA!
I HAD A DREAM ABOUT HER, LAST WEEK
A DRY ONE

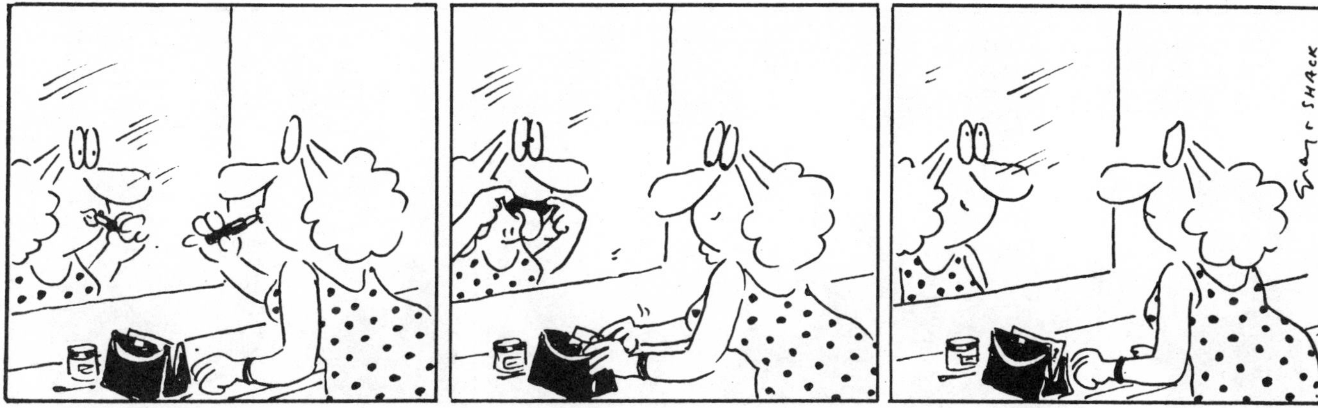

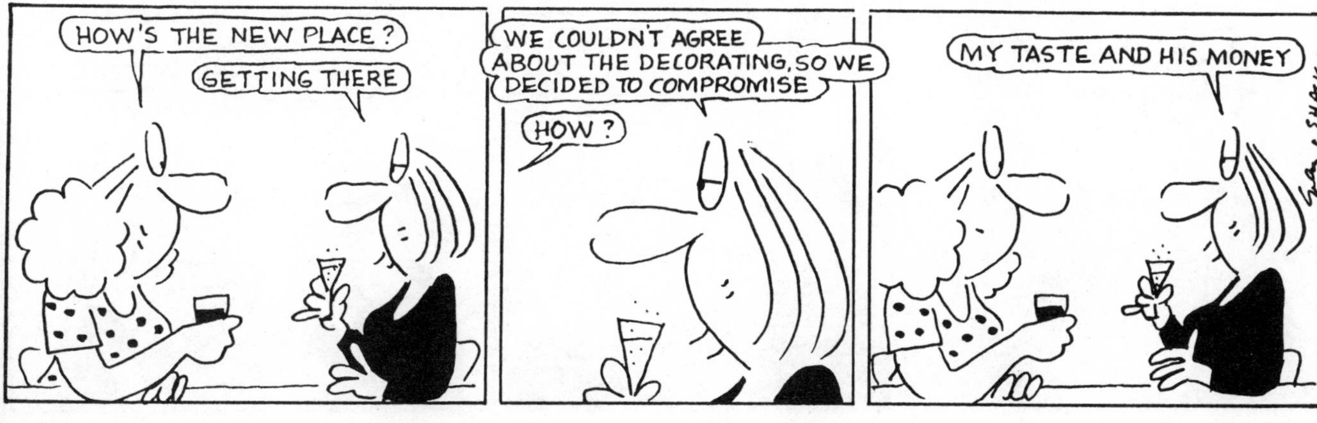
HOW'S THE NEW PLACE?
GETTING THERE
WE COULDN'T AGREE ABOUT THE DECORATING, SO WE DECIDED TO COMPROMISE
HOW?
MY TASTE AND HIS MONEY

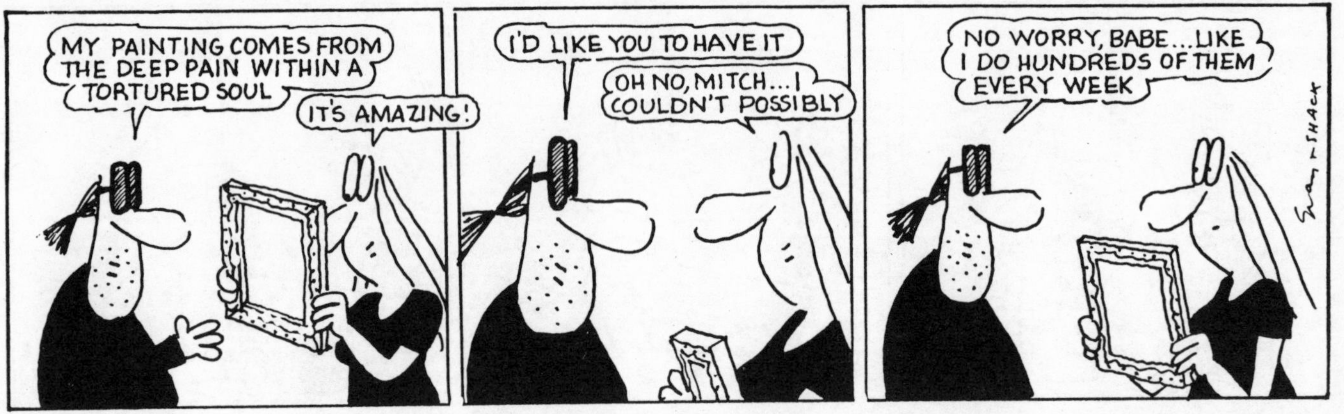
MY PAINTING COMES FROM THE DEEP PAIN WITHIN A TORTURED SOUL
IT'S AMAZING!
I'D LIKE YOU TO HAVE IT
OH NO, MITCH... I COULDN'T POSSIBLY
NO WORRY, BABE... LIKE I DO HUNDREDS OF THEM EVERY WEEK

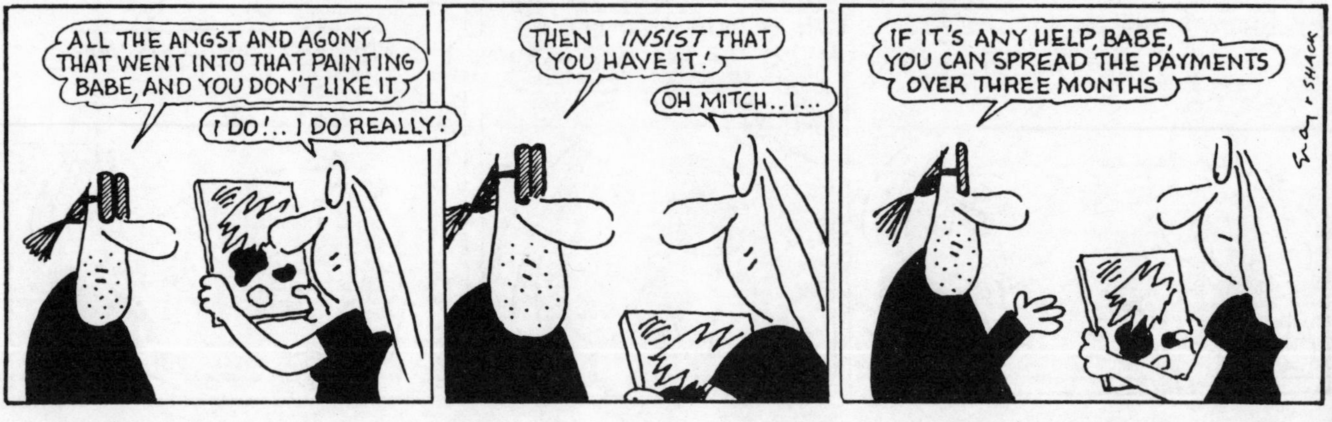
ALL THE ANGST AND AGONY THAT WENT INTO THAT PAINTING BABE, AND YOU DON'T LIKE IT
I DO!... I DO REALLY!
THEN I INSIST THAT YOU HAVE IT!
OH MITCH.. I...
IF IT'S ANY HELP, BABE, YOU CAN SPREAD THE PAYMENTS OVER THREE MONTHS

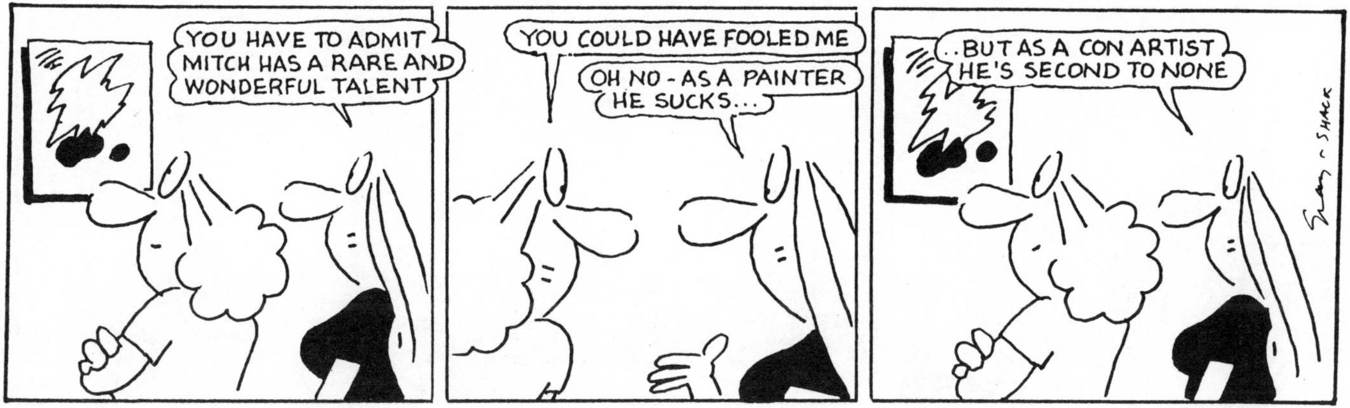
YOU HAVE TO ADMIT MITCH HAS A RARE AND WONDERFUL TALENT
YOU COULD HAVE FOOLED ME
OH NO - AS A PAINTER HE SUCKS...
..BUT AS A CON ARTIST HE'S SECOND TO NONE

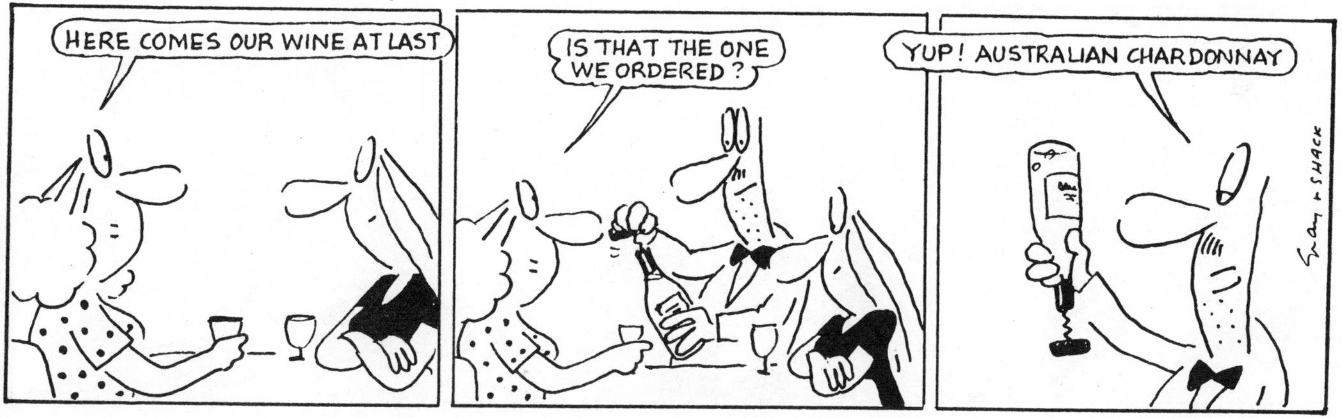
HERE COMES OUR WINE AT LAST
IS THAT THE ONE WE ORDERED ?
YUP! AUSTRALIAN CHARDONNAY

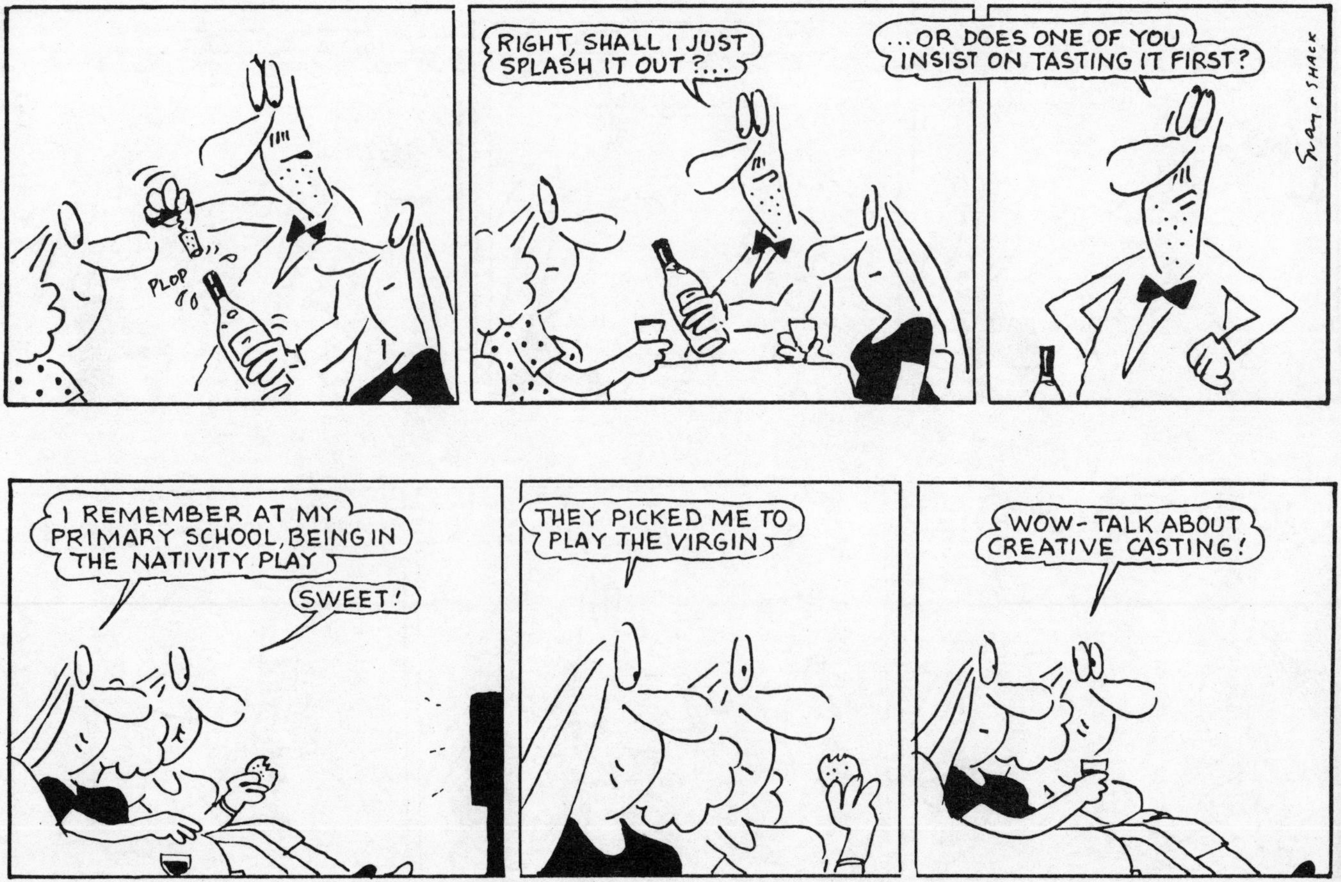
PLOP
RIGHT, SHALL I JUST SPLASH IT OUT?...
...OR DOES ONE OF YOU INSIST ON TASTING IT FIRST?
I REMEMBER AT MY PRIMARY SCHOOL, BEING IN THE NATIVITY PLAY
SWEET!
THEY PICKED ME TO PLAY THE VIRGIN
WOW - TALK ABOUT CREATIVE CASTING!

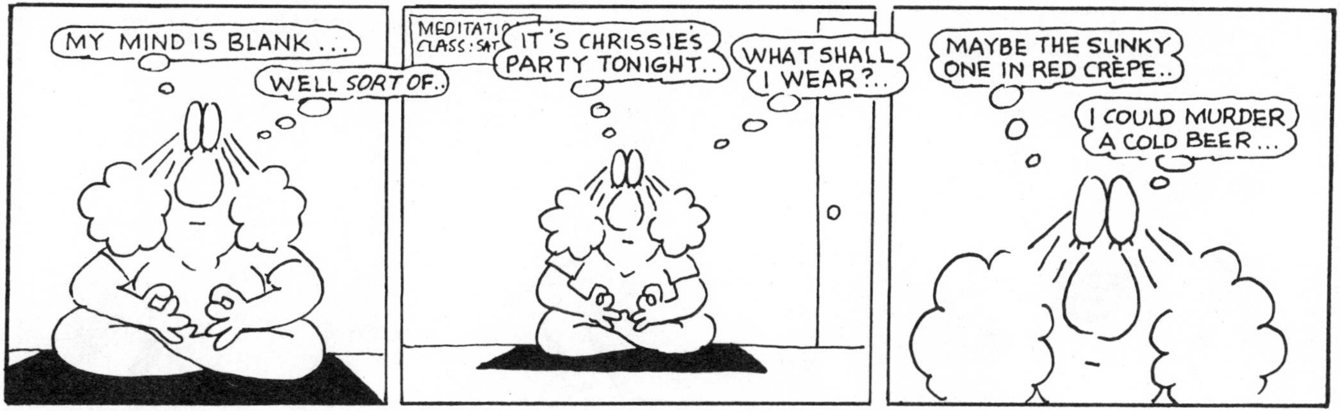
MY MIND IS BLANK . . .
WELL *SORT OF*..
MEDITATIO
CLASS : SAT
IT'S CHRISSIE'S PARTY TONIGHT..
WHAT SHALL I WEAR?..
MAYBE THE SLINKY ONE IN RED CRÈPE..
I COULD MURDER A COLD BEER . . .

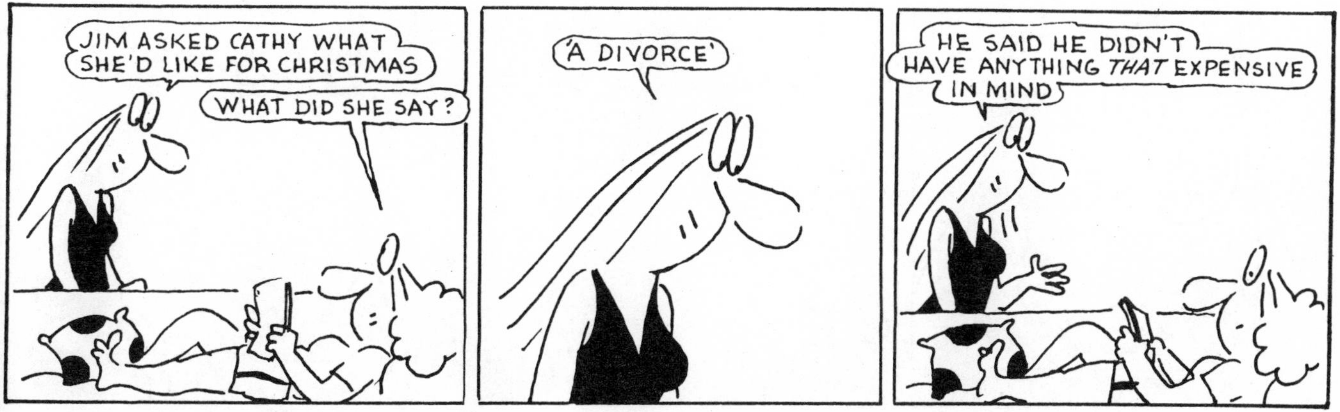
JIM ASKED CATHY WHAT SHE'D LIKE FOR CHRISTMAS
WHAT DID SHE SAY?
'A DIVORCE'
HE SAID HE DIDN'T HAVE ANYTHING *THAT* EXPENSIVE IN MIND

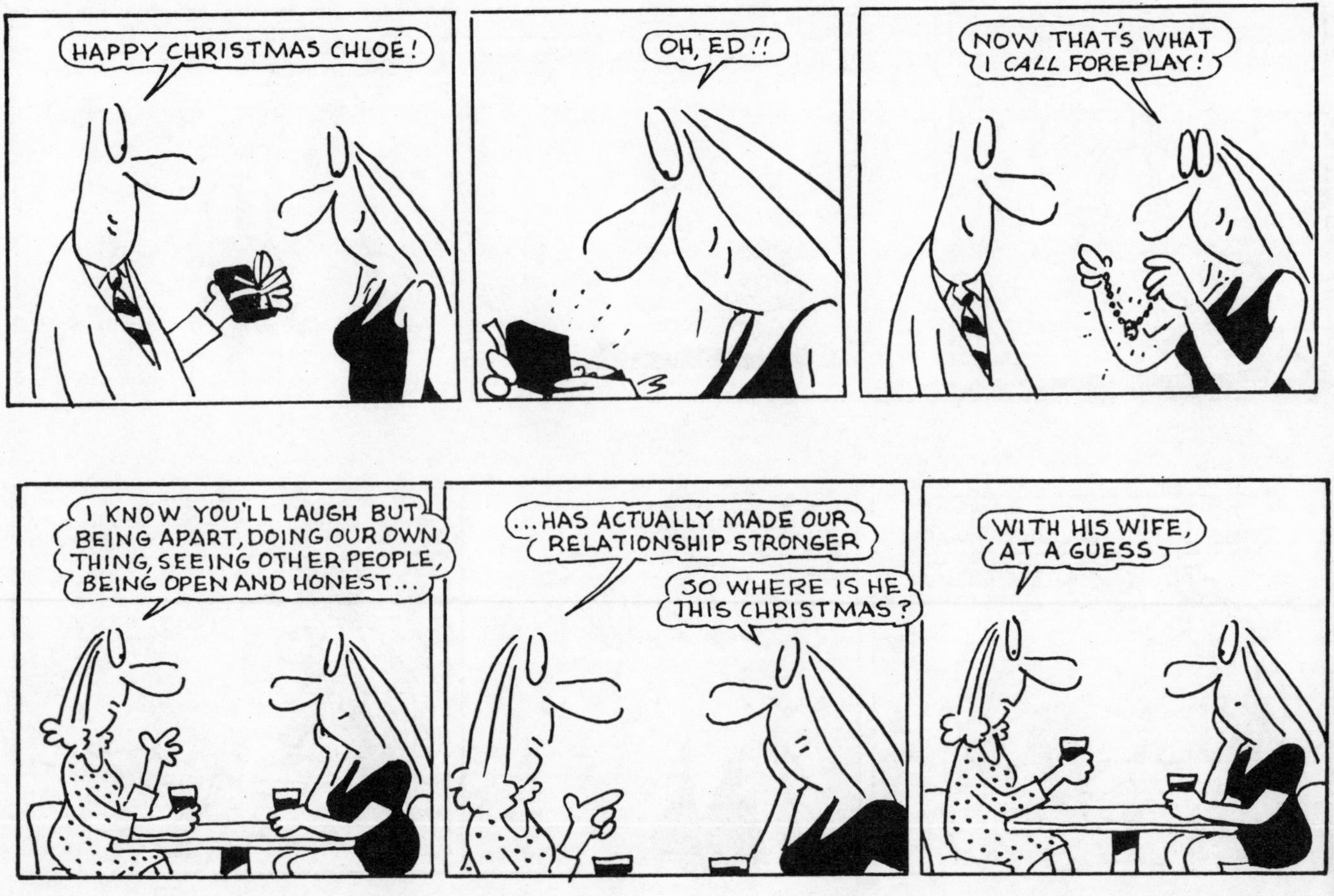

HAPPY CHRISTMAS CHLOÉ!
OH, ED!!
NOW THAT'S WHAT I CALL FOREPLAY!
I KNOW YOU'LL LAUGH BUT BEING APART, DOING OUR OWN THING, SEEING OTHER PEOPLE, BEING OPEN AND HONEST...
...HAS ACTUALLY MADE OUR RELATIONSHIP STRONGER
SO WHERE IS HE THIS CHRISTMAS?
WITH HIS WIFE, AT A GUESS

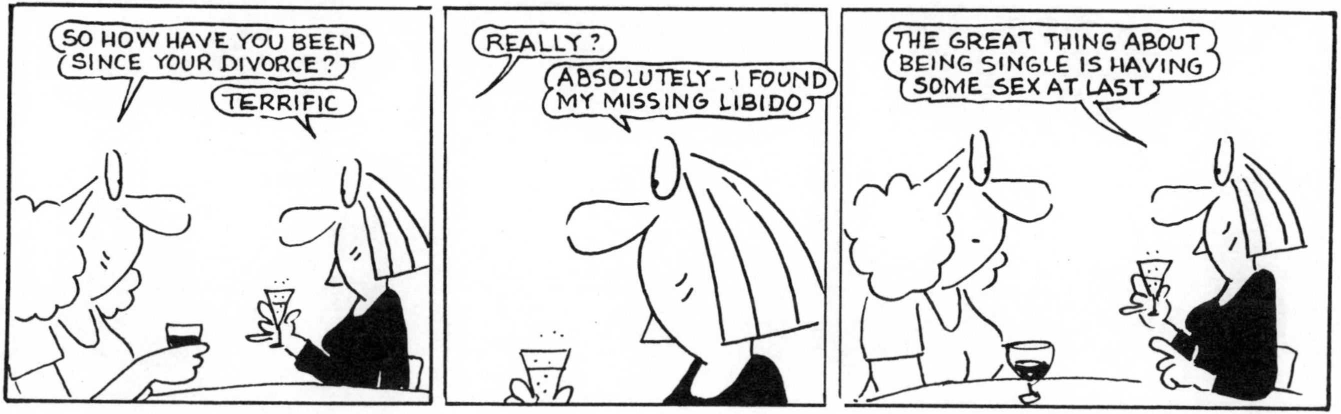
SO HOW HAVE YOU BEEN SINCE YOUR DIVORCE?
TERRIFIC
REALLY?
ABSOLUTELY - I FOUND MY MISSING LIBIDO
THE GREAT THING ABOUT BEING SINGLE IS HAVING SOME SEX AT LAST

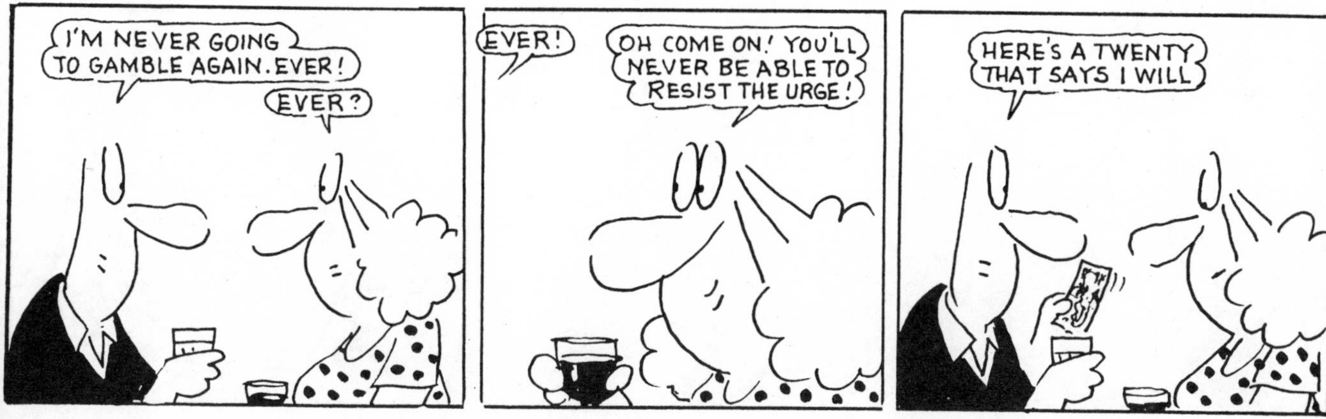
I'M NEVER GOING TO GAMBLE AGAIN. EVER!
EVER?
EVER!
OH COME ON! YOU'LL NEVER BE ABLE TO RESIST THE URGE!
HERE'S A TWENTY THAT SAYS I WILL

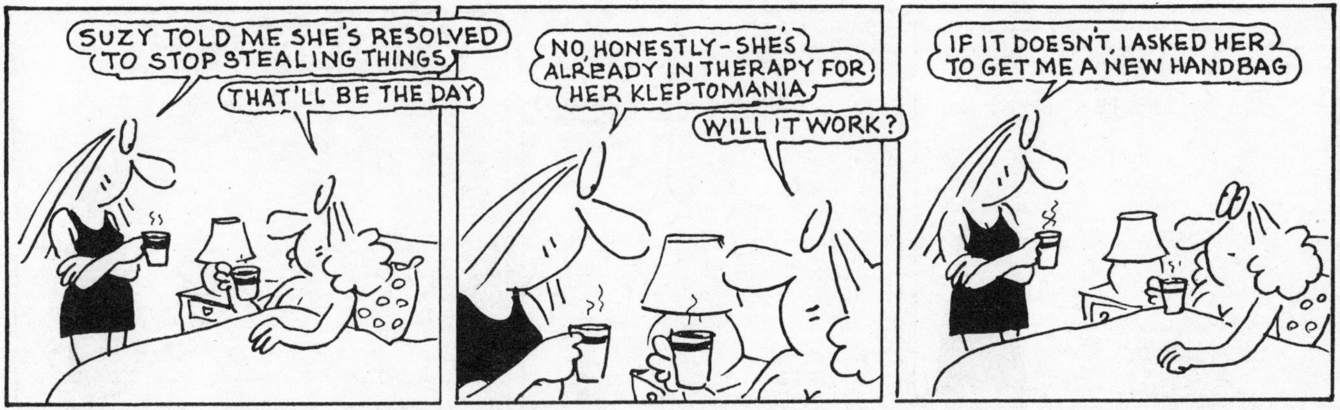
SUZY TOLD ME SHE'S RESOLVED TO STOP STEALING THINGS
THAT'LL BE THE DAY
NO, HONESTLY - SHE'S ALREADY IN THERAPY FOR HER KLEPTOMANIA
WILL IT WORK?
IF IT DOESN'T, I ASKED HER TO GET ME A NEW HANDBAG

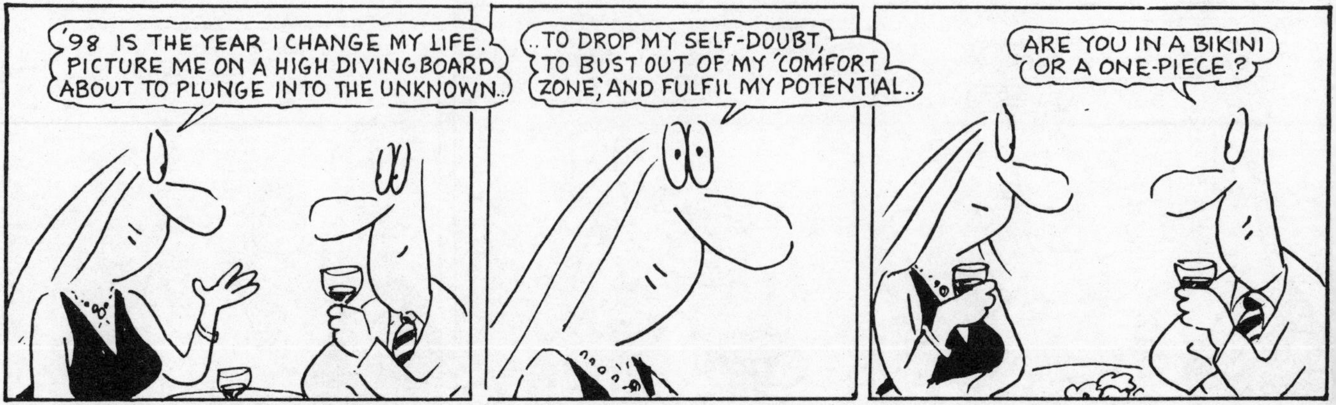
'98 IS THE YEAR I CHANGE MY LIFE. PICTURE ME ON A HIGH DIVING BOARD ABOUT TO PLUNGE INTO THE UNKNOWN..
..TO DROP MY SELF-DOUBT, TO BUST OUT OF MY 'COMFORT ZONE,' AND FULFIL MY POTENTIAL..
ARE YOU IN A BIKINI OR A ONE-PIECE?

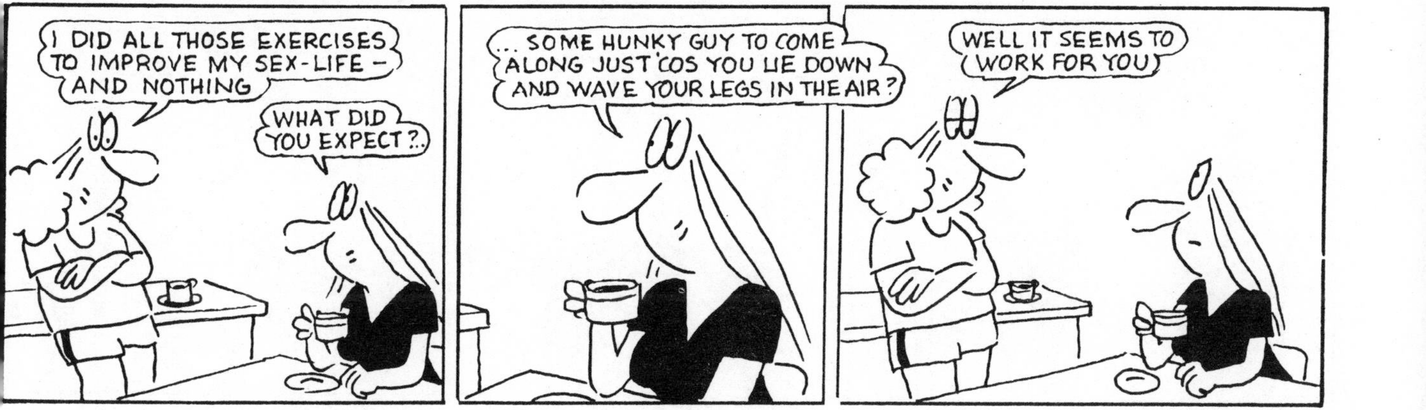
I DID ALL THOSE EXERCISES TO IMPROVE MY SEX-LIFE – AND NOTHING
WHAT DID YOU EXPECT?..
... SOME HUNKY GUY TO COME ALONG JUST 'COS YOU LIE DOWN AND WAVE YOUR LEGS IN THE AIR?
WELL IT SEEMS TO WORK FOR YOU

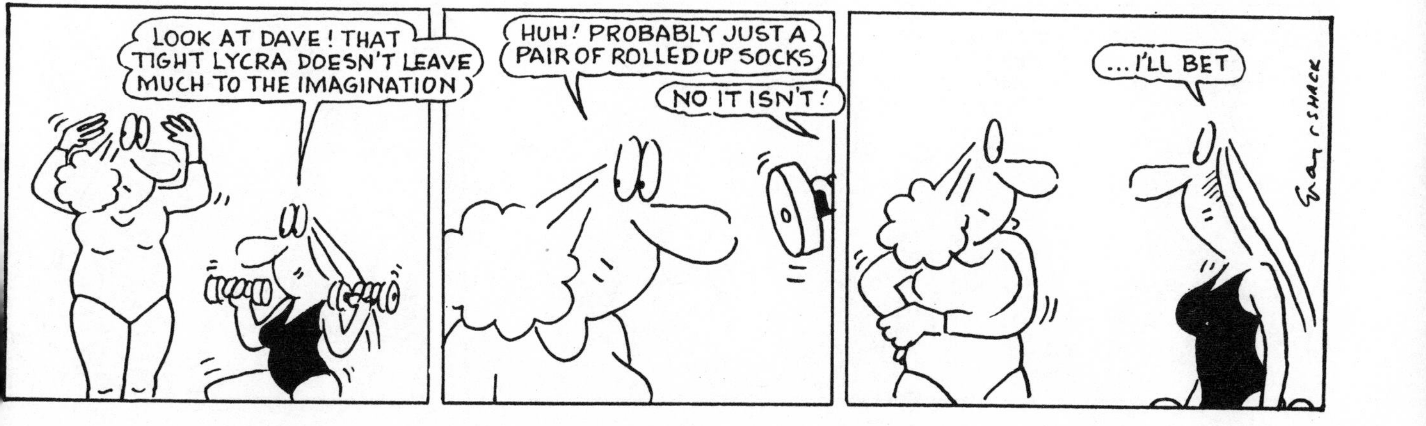
LOOK AT DAVE! THAT TIGHT LYCRA DOESN'T LEAVE MUCH TO THE IMAGINATION
HUH! PROBABLY JUST A PAIR OF ROLLED UP SOCKS
NO IT ISN'T!
... I'LL BET

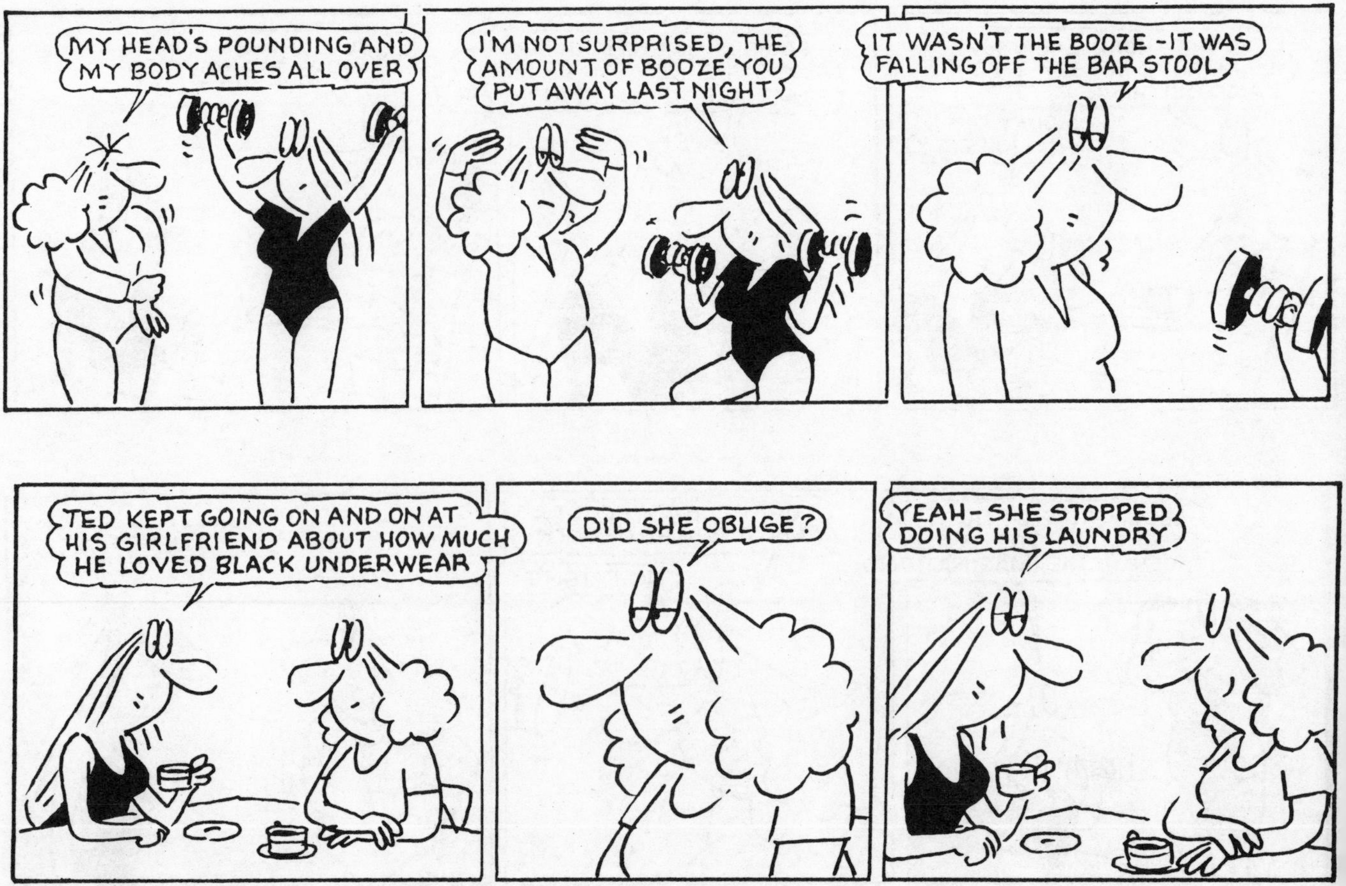
MY HEAD'S POUNDING AND MY BODY ACHES ALL OVER
I'M NOT SURPRISED, THE AMOUNT OF BOOZE YOU PUT AWAY LAST NIGHT
IT WASN'T THE BOOZE - IT WAS FALLING OFF THE BAR STOOL
TED KEPT GOING ON AND ON AT HIS GIRLFRIEND ABOUT HOW MUCH HE LOVED BLACK UNDERWEAR
DID SHE OBLIGE?
YEAH - SHE STOPPED DOING HIS LAUNDRY

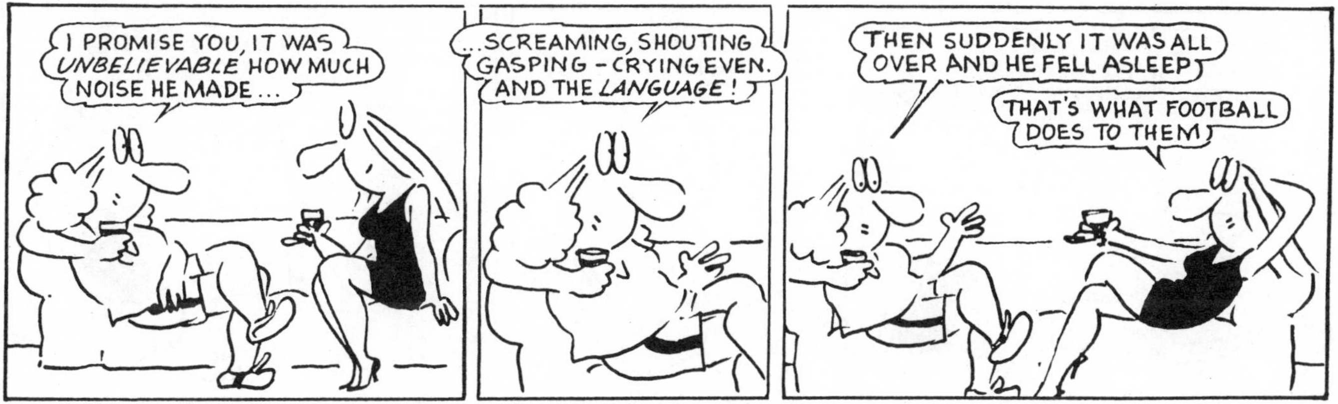
I PROMISE YOU, IT WAS *UNBELIEVABLE* HOW MUCH NOISE HE MADE...
...SCREAMING, SHOUTING GASPING - CRYING EVEN. AND THE *LANGUAGE*!
THEN SUDDENLY IT WAS ALL OVER AND HE FELL ASLEEP
THAT'S WHAT FOOTBALL DOES TO THEM

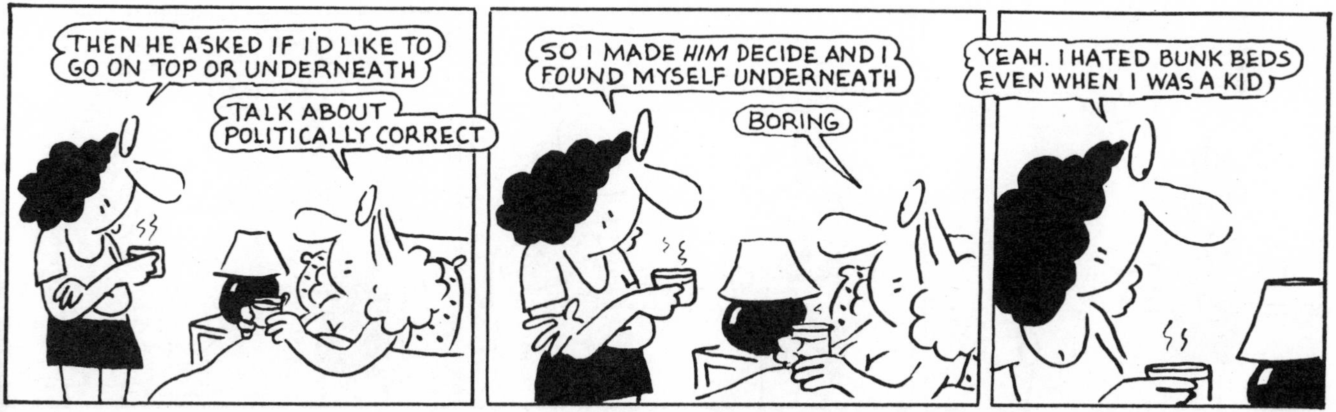
THEN HE ASKED IF I'D LIKE TO GO ON TOP OR UNDERNEATH
TALK ABOUT POLITICALLY CORRECT
SO I MADE *HIM* DECIDE AND I FOUND MYSELF UNDERNEATH
BORING
YEAH. I HATED BUNK BEDS EVEN WHEN I WAS A KID

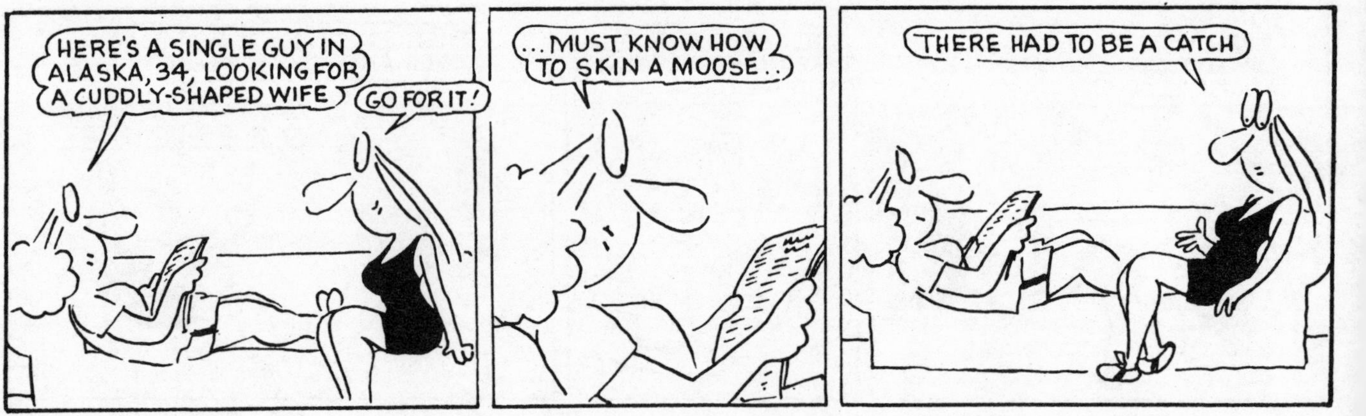
HERE'S A SINGLE GUY IN ALASKA, 34, LOOKING FOR A CUDDLY-SHAPED WIFE
GO FOR IT!
...MUST KNOW HOW TO SKIN A MOOSE..
THERE HAD TO BE A CATCH

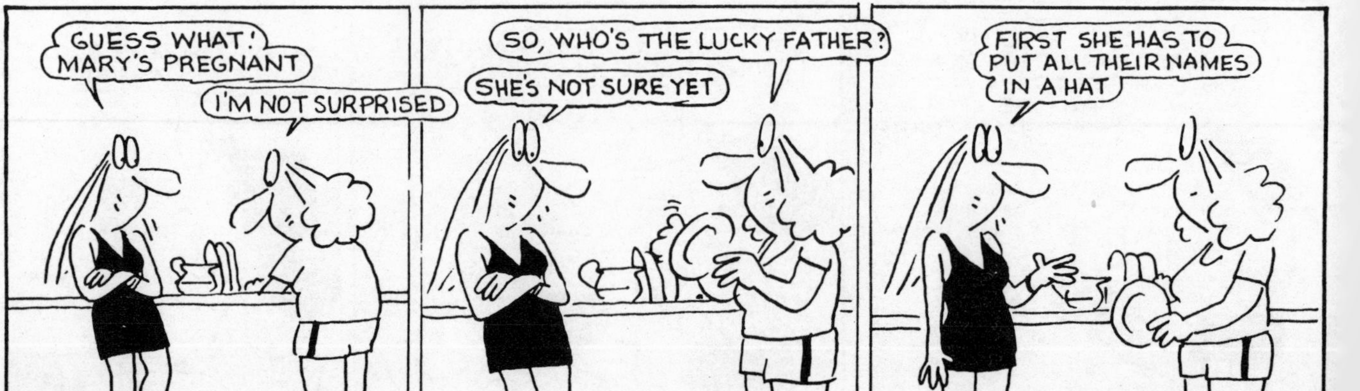
GUESS WHAT! MARY'S PREGNANT
I'M NOT SURPRISED
SO, WHO'S THE LUCKY FATHER?
SHE'S NOT SURE YET
FIRST SHE HAS TO PUT ALL THEIR NAMES IN A HAT

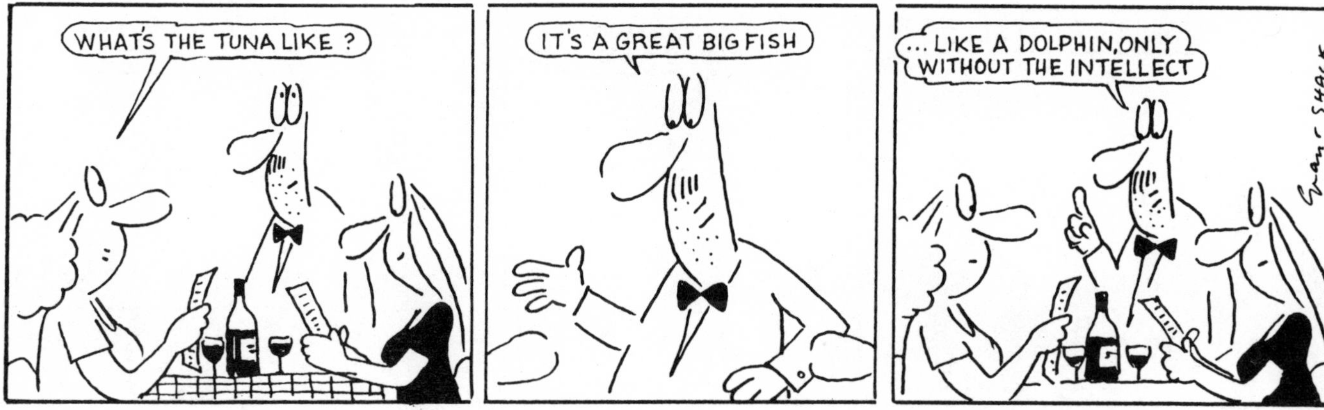
WHAT'S THE TUNA LIKE ?
IT'S A GREAT BIG FISH
... LIKE A DOLPHIN, ONLY WITHOUT THE INTELLECT

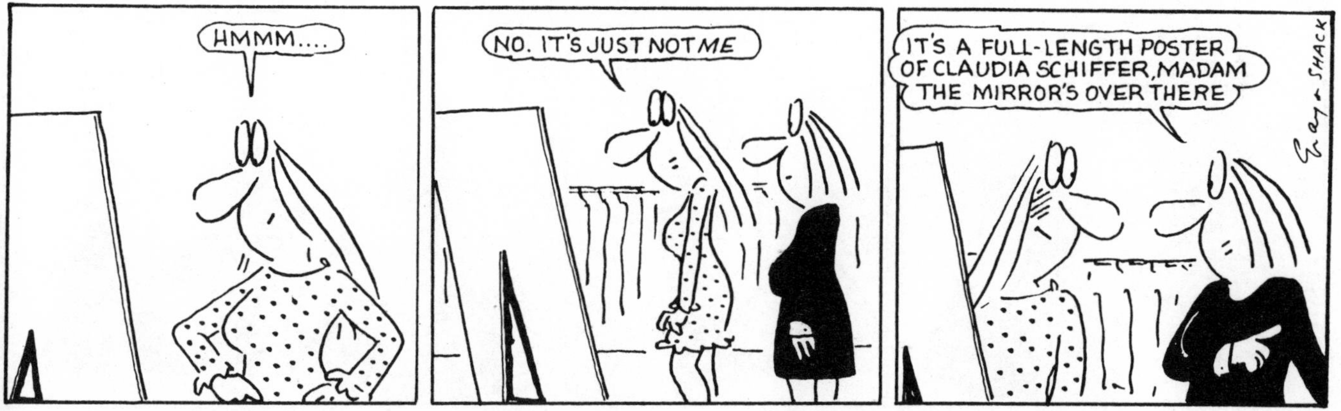
HMMM....
NO. IT'S JUST NOT *ME*
IT'S A FULL-LENGTH POSTER OF CLAUDIA SCHIFFER, MADAM THE MIRROR'S OVER THERE

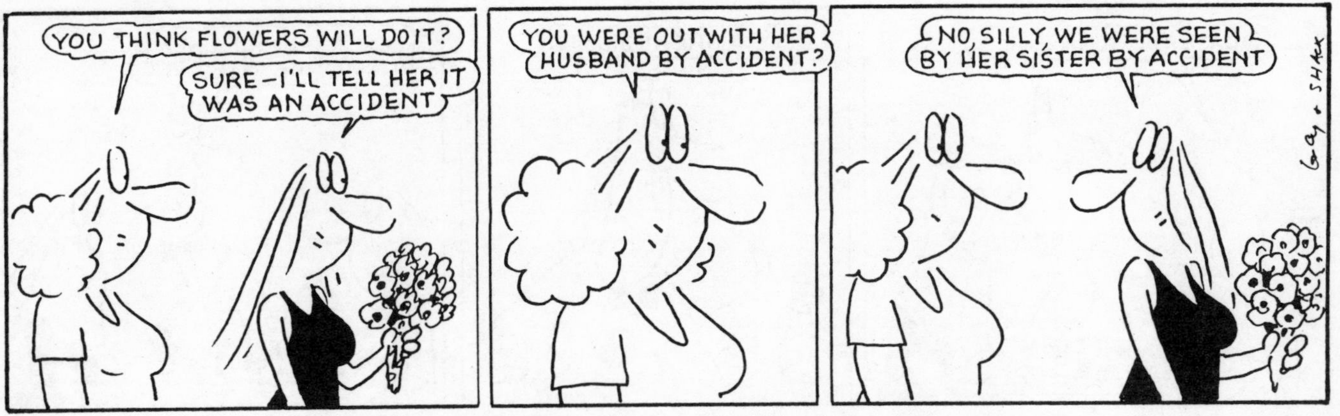
YOU THINK FLOWERS WILL DO IT?
SURE – I'LL TELL HER IT WAS AN ACCIDENT
YOU WERE OUT WITH HER HUSBAND BY ACCIDENT?
NO, SILLY, WE WERE SEEN BY HER SISTER BY ACCIDENT

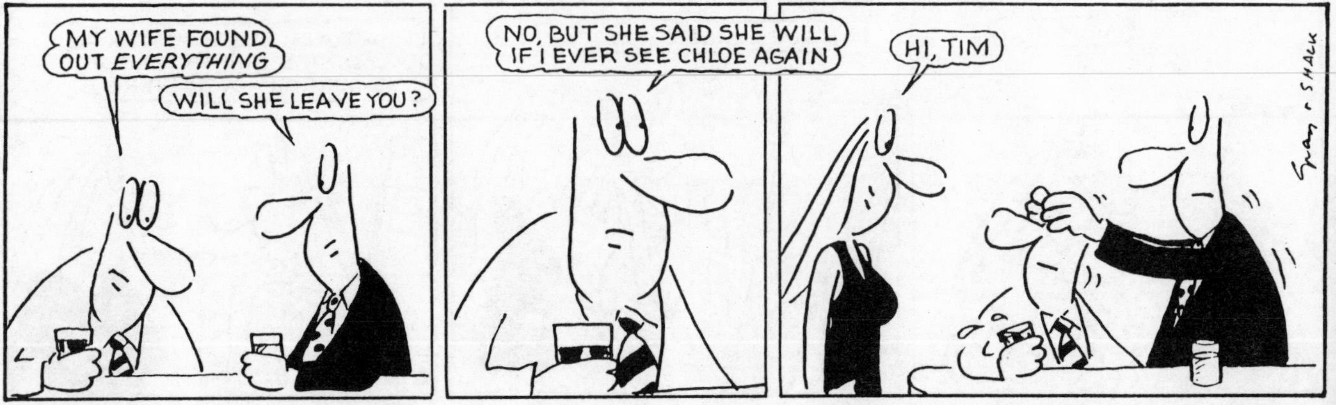
MY WIFE FOUND OUT *EVERYTHING*
WILL SHE LEAVE YOU?
NO, BUT SHE SAID SHE WILL IF I EVER SEE CHLOE AGAIN
HI, TIM

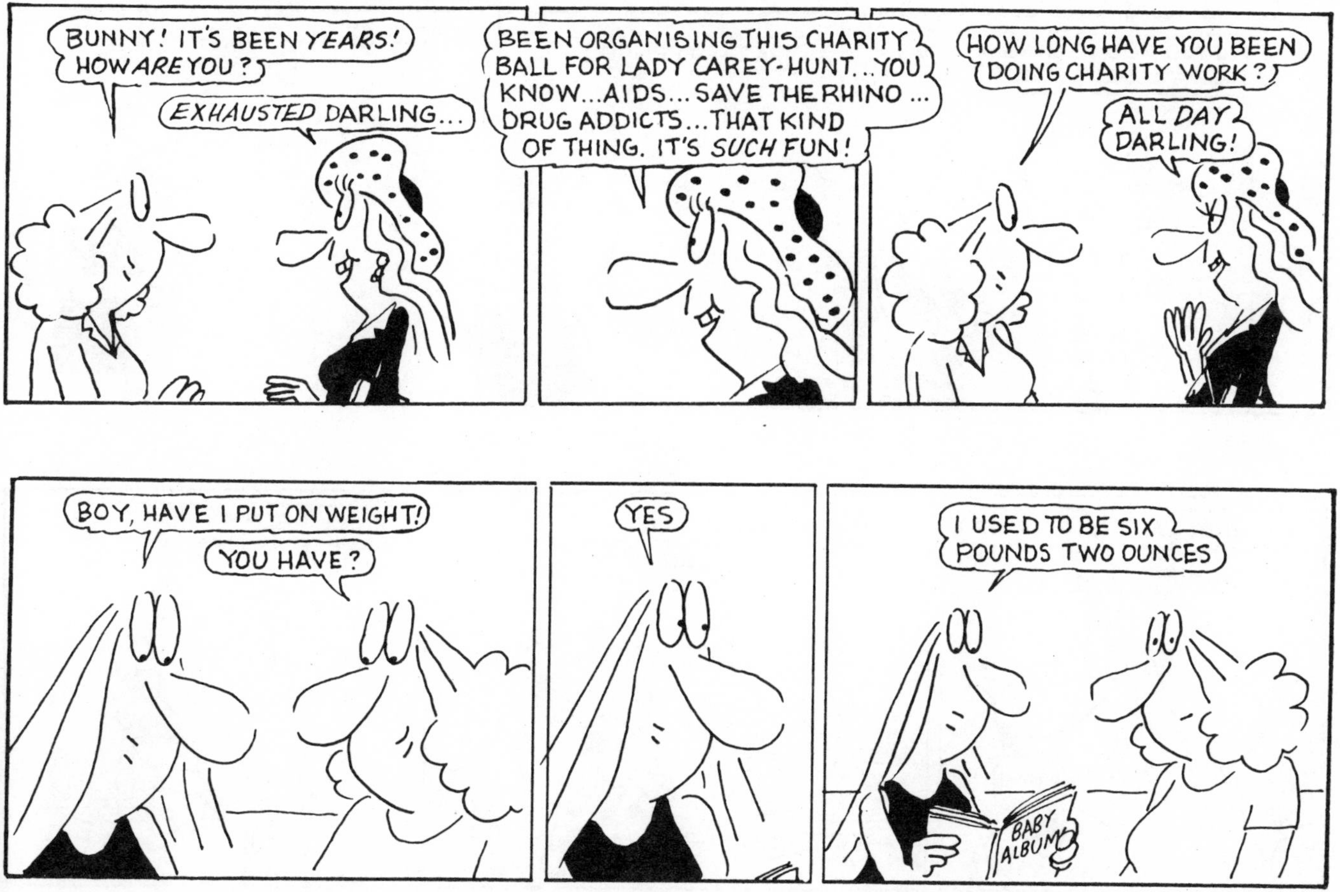
BUNNY! IT'S BEEN *YEARS!* HOW *ARE* YOU?
EXHAUSTED DARLING...
BEEN ORGANISING THIS CHARITY BALL FOR LADY CAREY-HUNT...YOU KNOW...AIDS... SAVE THE RHINO... DRUG ADDICTS...THAT KIND OF THING. IT'S *SUCH* FUN!
HOW LONG HAVE YOU BEEN DOING CHARITY WORK?
ALL *DAY* DARLING!
BOY, HAVE I PUT ON WEIGHT!
YOU HAVE?
YES
I USED TO BE SIX POUNDS TWO OUNCES
BABY ALBUM

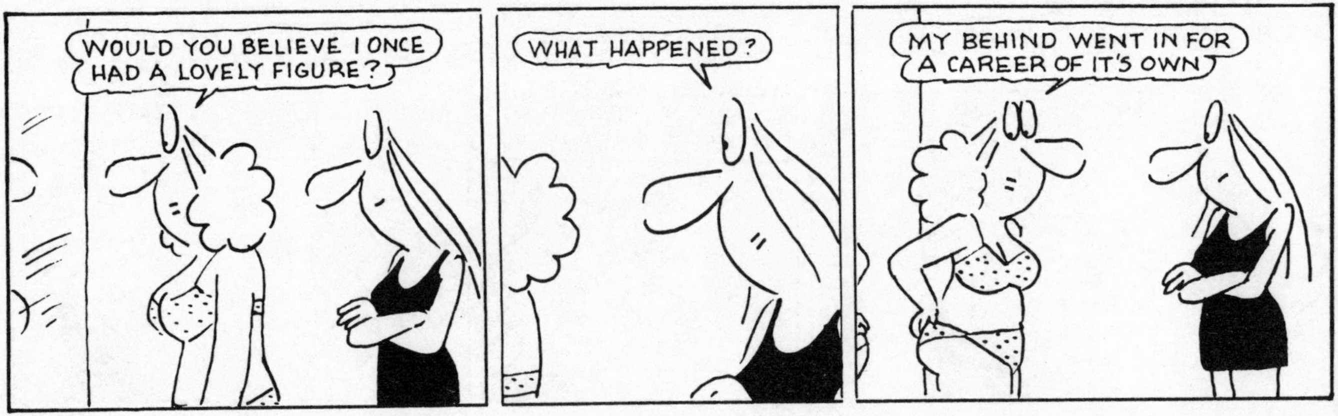
WOULD YOU BELIEVE I ONCE HAD A LOVELY FIGURE?
WHAT HAPPENED?
MY BEHIND WENT IN FOR A CAREER OF IT'S OWN

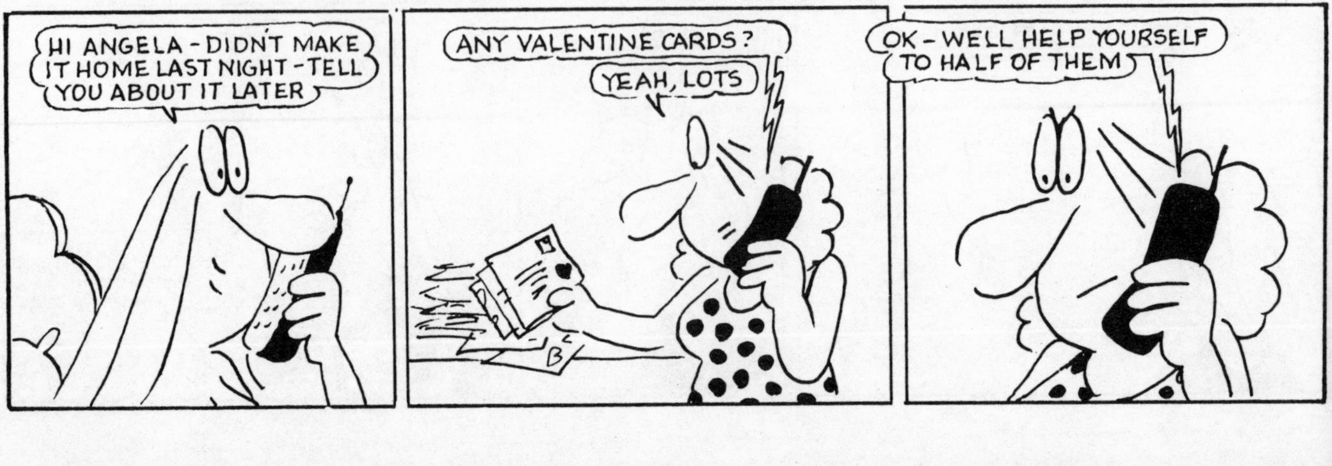
HI ANGELA - DIDN'T MAKE IT HOME LAST NIGHT - TELL YOU ABOUT IT LATER
ANY VALENTINE CARDS?
YEAH, LOTS
OK - WELL HELP YOURSELF TO HALF OF THEM

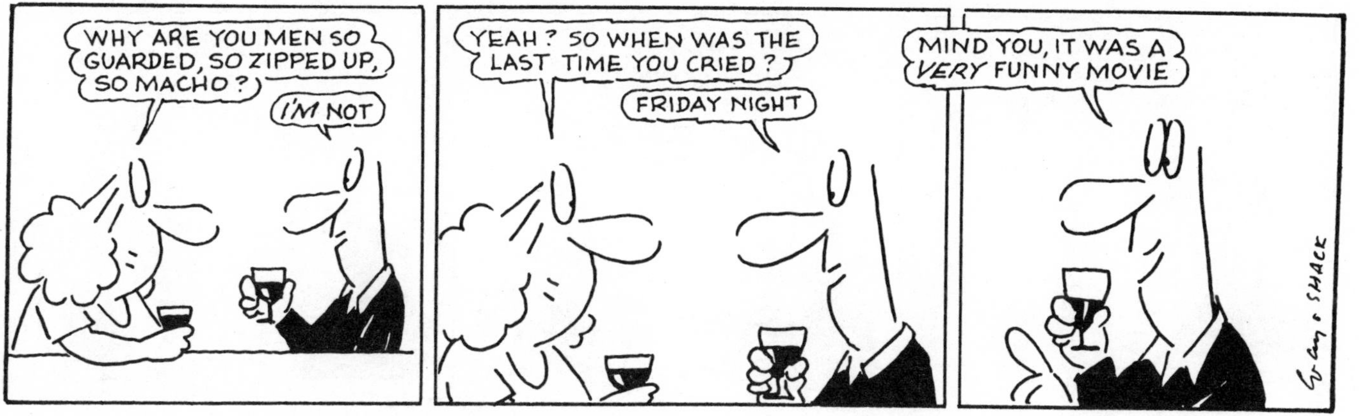
WHY ARE YOU MEN SO GUARDED, SO ZIPPED UP, SO MACHO?
I'M NOT
YEAH? SO WHEN WAS THE LAST TIME YOU CRIED?
FRIDAY NIGHT
MIND YOU, IT WAS A *VERY* FUNNY MOVIE

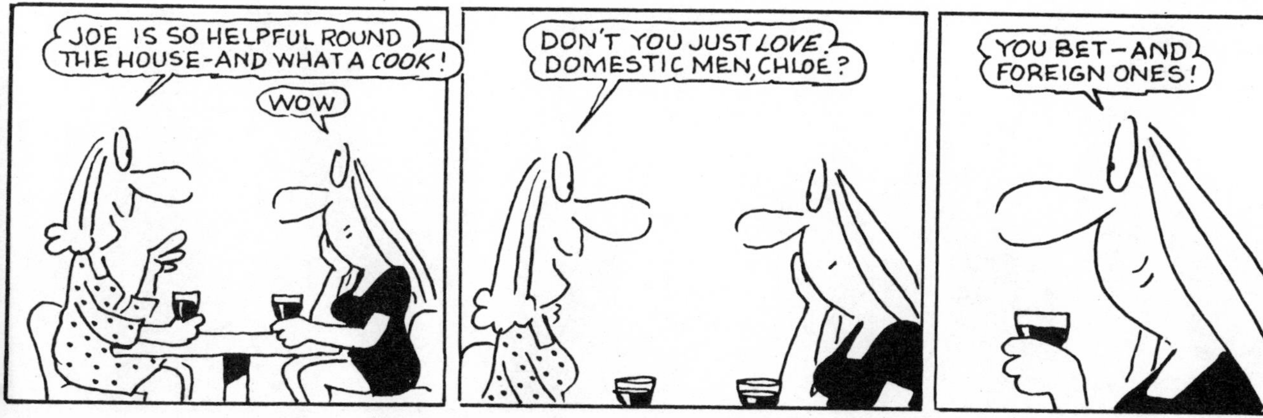
JOE IS SO HELPFUL ROUND THE HOUSE-AND WHAT A *COOK*!
WOW
DON'T YOU JUST *LOVE* DOMESTIC MEN, CHLOE?
YOU BET-AND FOREIGN ONES!

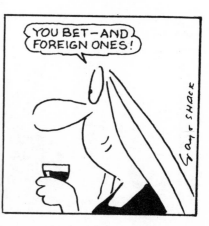

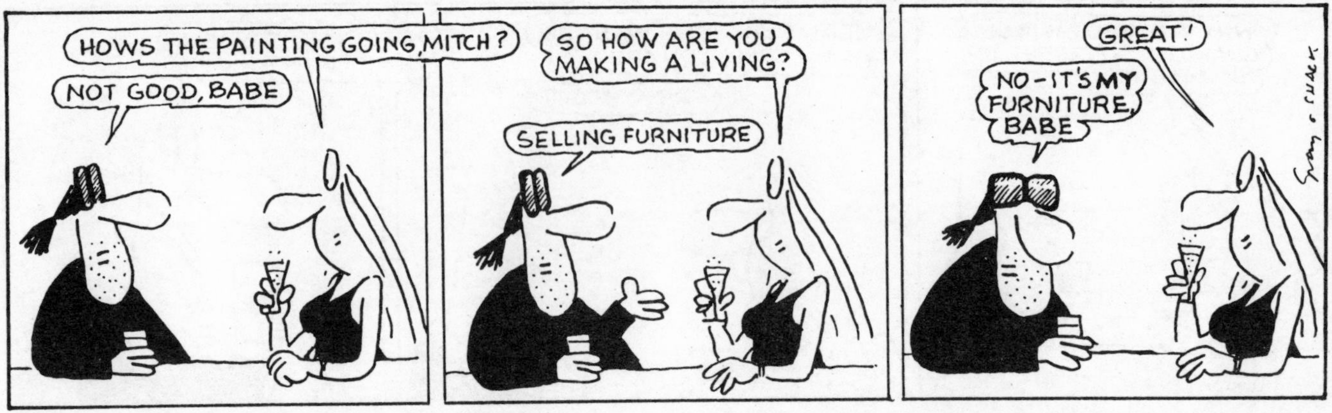
HOWS THE PAINTING GOING, MITCH?
NOT GOOD, BABE
SO HOW ARE YOU MAKING A LIVING?
SELLING FURNITURE
GREAT!
NO - IT'S MY FURNITURE, BABE

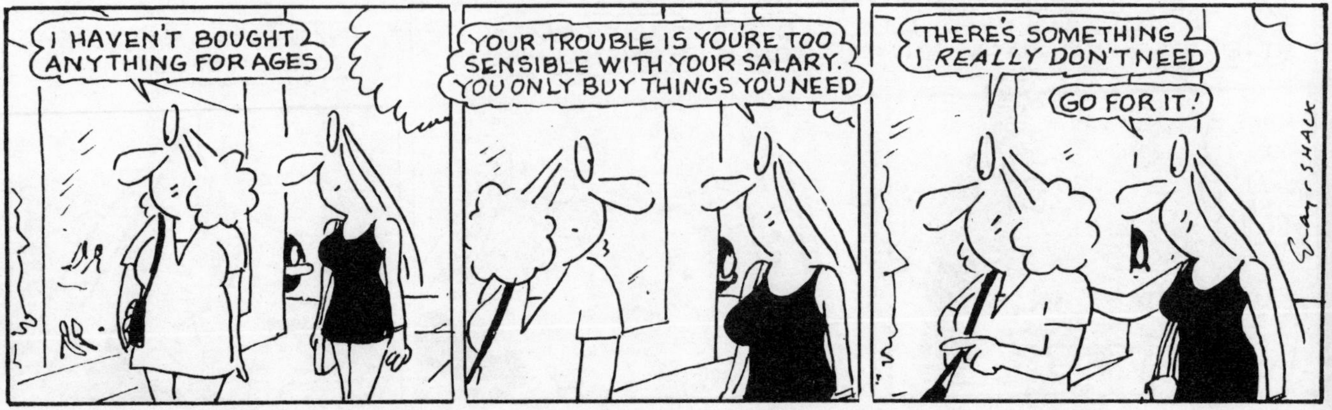
I HAVEN'T BOUGHT ANYTHING FOR AGES
YOUR TROUBLE IS YOU'RE TOO SENSIBLE WITH YOUR SALARY. YOU ONLY BUY THINGS YOU NEED
THERE'S SOMETHING I *REALLY* DON'T NEED
GO FOR IT!

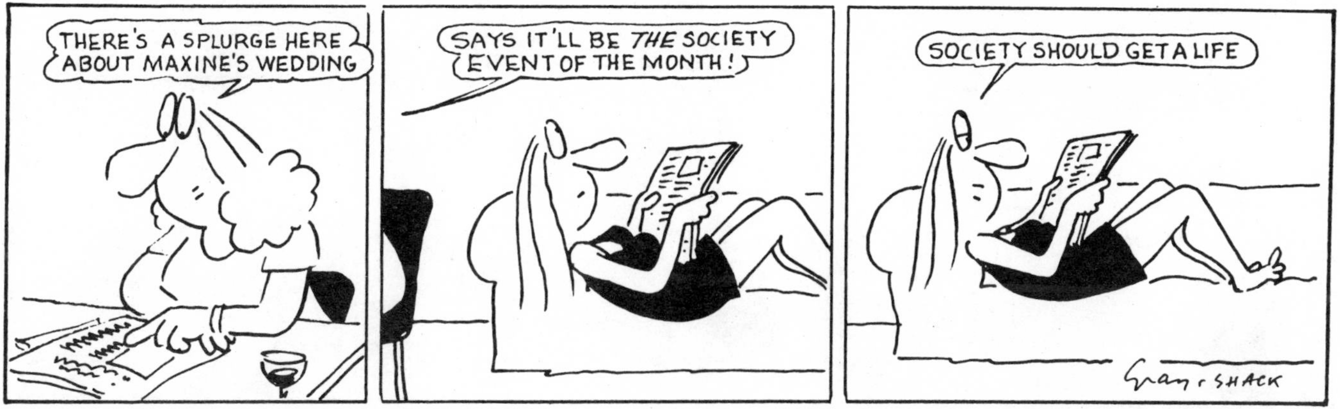
THERE'S A SPLURGE HERE ABOUT MAXINE'S WEDDING
SAYS IT'LL BE *THE* SOCIETY EVENT OF THE MONTH!
SOCIETY SHOULD GET A LIFE

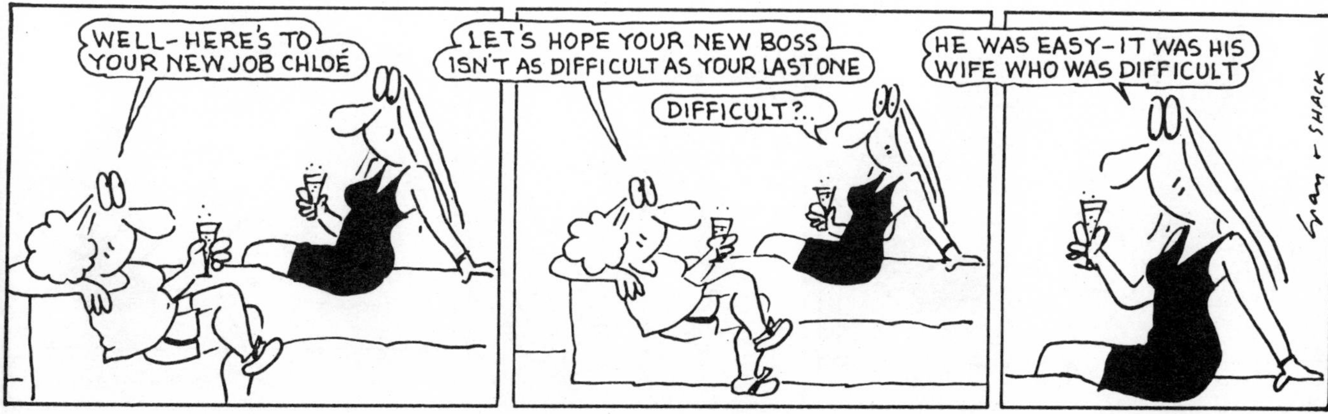
WELL-HERE'S TO YOUR NEW JOB CHLOÉ
LET'S HOPE YOUR NEW BOSS ISN'T AS DIFFICULT AS YOUR LAST ONE
DIFFICULT?..
HE WAS EASY-IT WAS HIS WIFE WHO WAS DIFFICULT

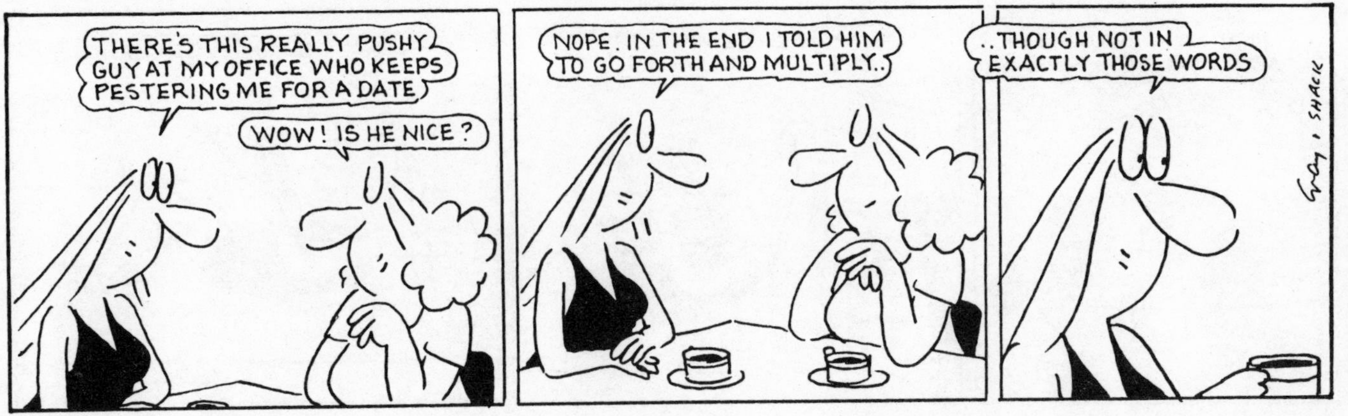
THERE'S THIS REALLY PUSHY GUY AT MY OFFICE WHO KEEPS PESTERING ME FOR A DATE
WOW! IS HE NICE?
NOPE. IN THE END I TOLD HIM TO GO FORTH AND MULTIPLY..
..THOUGH NOT IN EXACTLY THOSE WORDS
Gray & SHACK

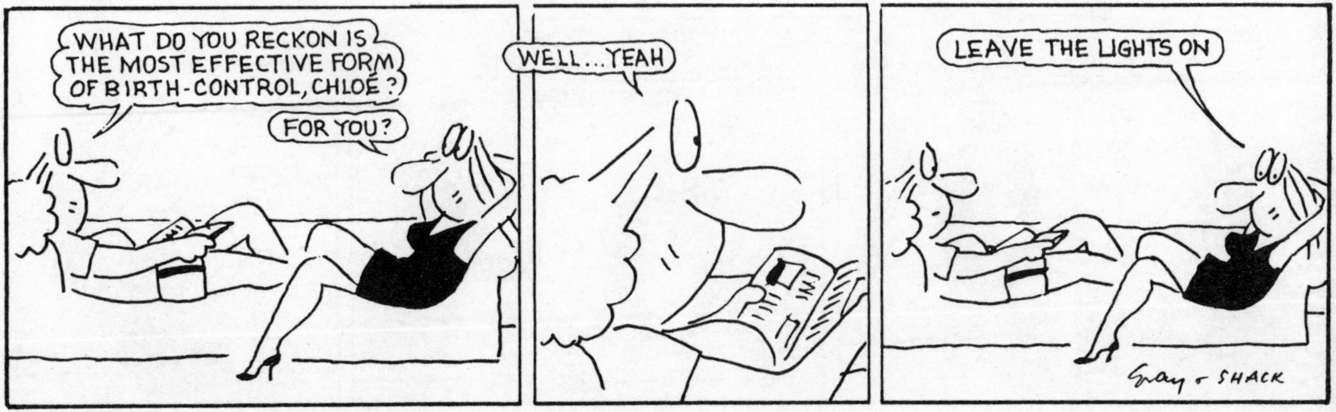
WHAT DO YOU RECKON IS THE MOST EFFECTIVE FORM OF BIRTH-CONTROL, CHLOÉ?
FOR YOU?
WELL...YEAH
LEAVE THE LIGHTS ON
Gray & SHACK

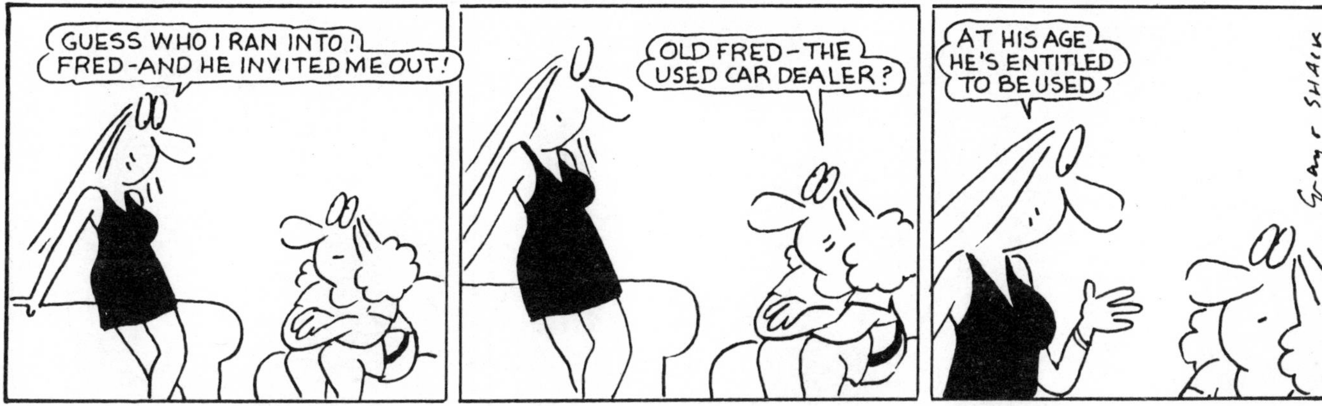
GUESS WHO I RAN INTO! FRED-AND HE INVITED ME OUT!
OLD FRED-THE USED CAR DEALER?
AT HIS AGE HE'S ENTITLED TO BE USED

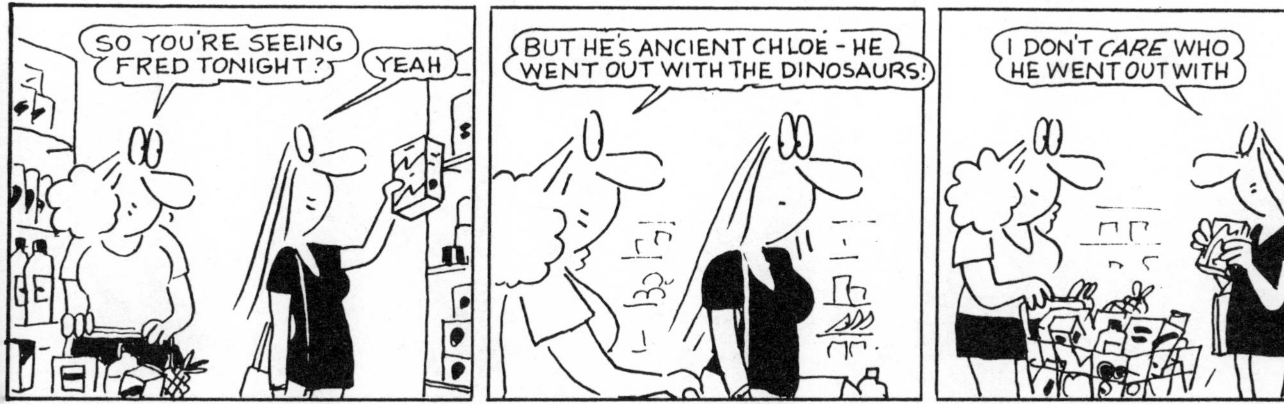
SO YOU'RE SEEING FRED TONIGHT?
YEAH
BUT HE'S ANCIENT CHLOE - HE WENT OUT WITH THE DINOSAURS!
I DON'T *CARE* WHO HE WENT OUT WITH

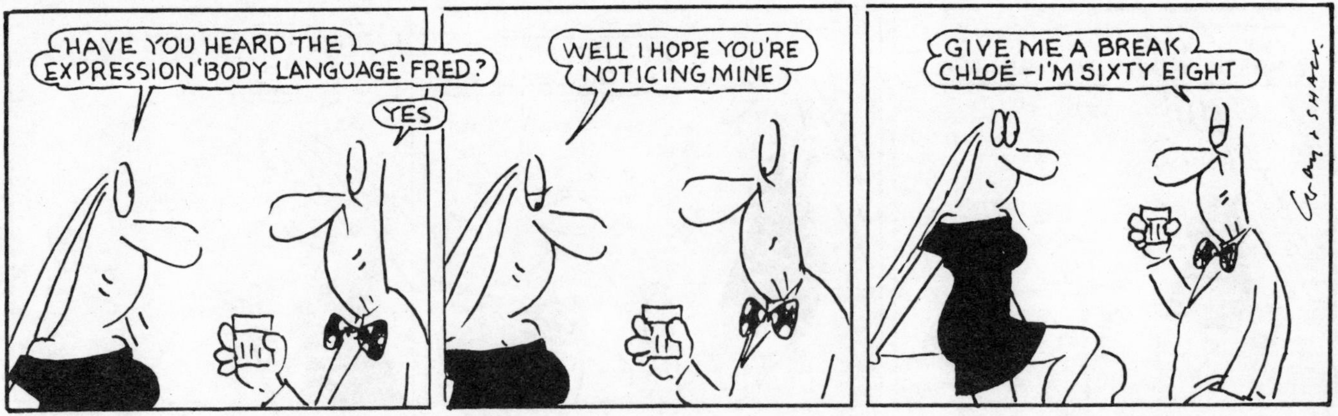
HAVE YOU HEARD THE EXPRESSION 'BODY LANGUAGE' FRED?
YES
WELL I HOPE YOU'RE NOTICING MINE
GIVE ME A BREAK CHLOÉ - I'M SIXTY EIGHT

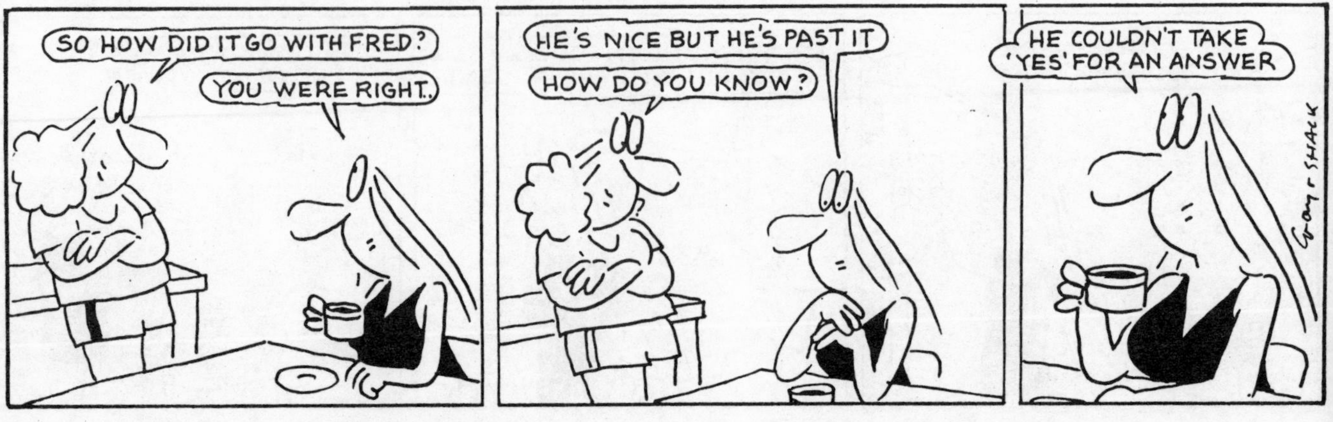
SO HOW DID IT GO WITH FRED?
YOU WERE RIGHT..
HE'S NICE BUT HE'S PAST IT
HOW DO YOU KNOW?
HE COULDN'T TAKE 'YES' FOR AN ANSWER

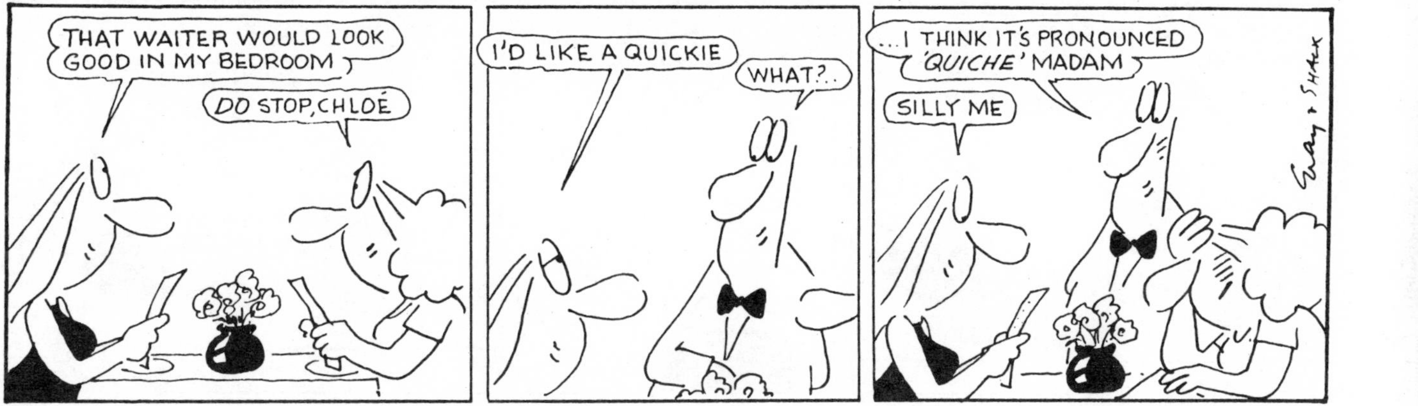
THAT WAITER WOULD LOOK GOOD IN MY BEDROOM
DO STOP, CHLOÉ
I'D LIKE A QUICKIE
WHAT?..
...I THINK IT'S PRONOUNCED 'QUICHE' MADAM
SILLY ME

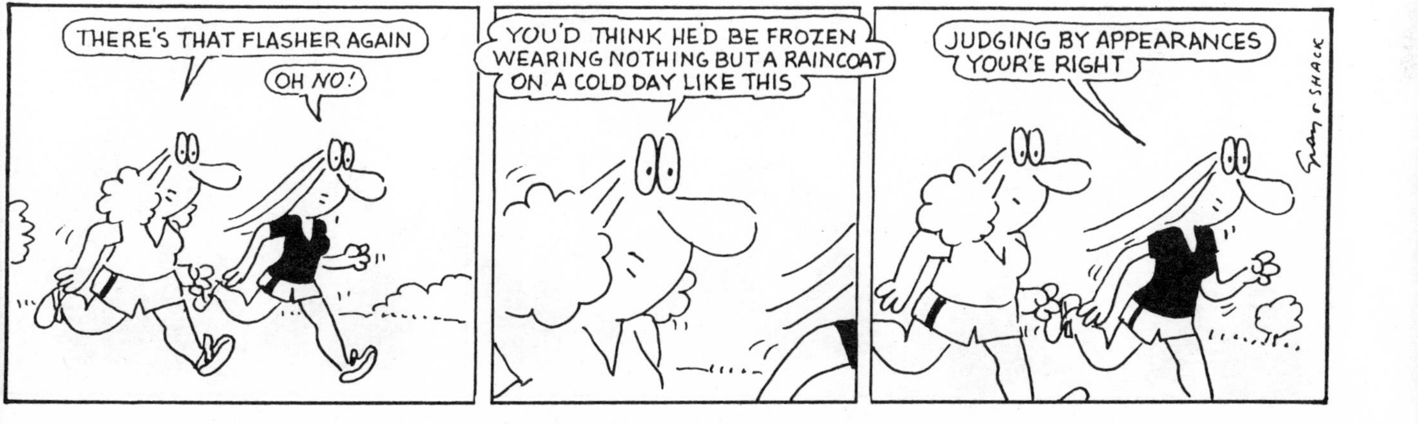
THERE'S THAT FLASHER AGAIN
OH NO!
YOU'D THINK HE'D BE FROZEN WEARING NOTHING BUT A RAINCOAT ON A COLD DAY LIKE THIS
JUDGING BY APPEARANCES YOUR'E RIGHT

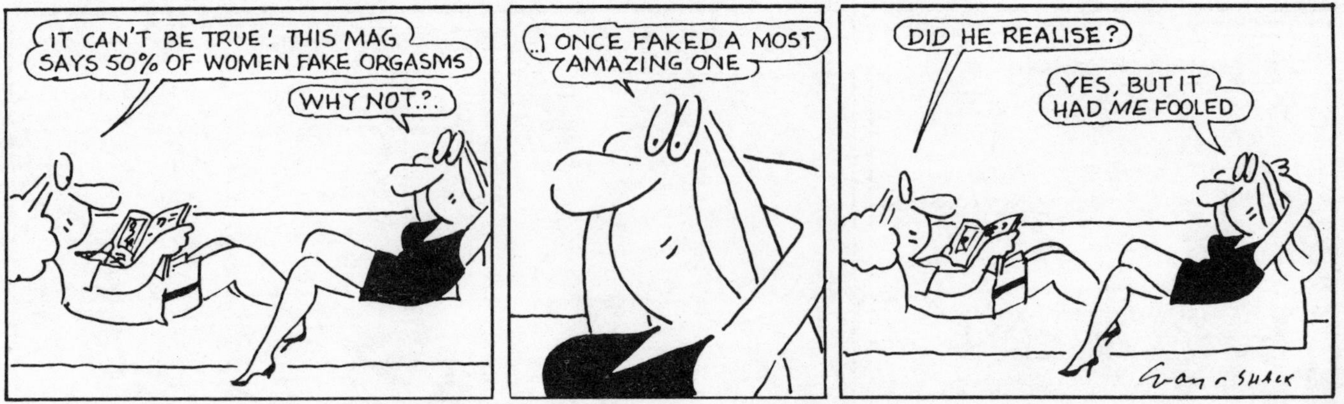
IT CAN'T BE TRUE! THIS MAG SAYS 50% OF WOMEN FAKE ORGASMS
WHY NOT.?.
..I ONCE FAKED A MOST AMAZING ONE
DID HE REALISE?
YES, BUT IT HAD *ME* FOOLED
Gray r SHACK

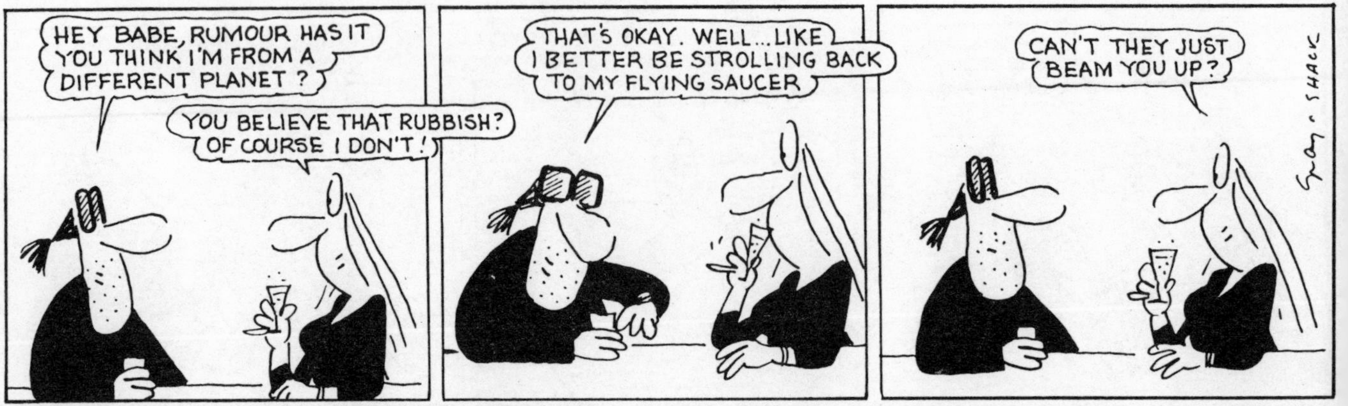
HEY BABE, RUMOUR HAS IT YOU THINK I'M FROM A DIFFERENT PLANET?
YOU BELIEVE THAT RUBBISH? OF COURSE I DON'T!
THAT'S OKAY. WELL... LIKE I BETTER BE STROLLING BACK TO MY FLYING SAUCER
CAN'T THEY JUST BEAM YOU UP?
Gray r SHACK

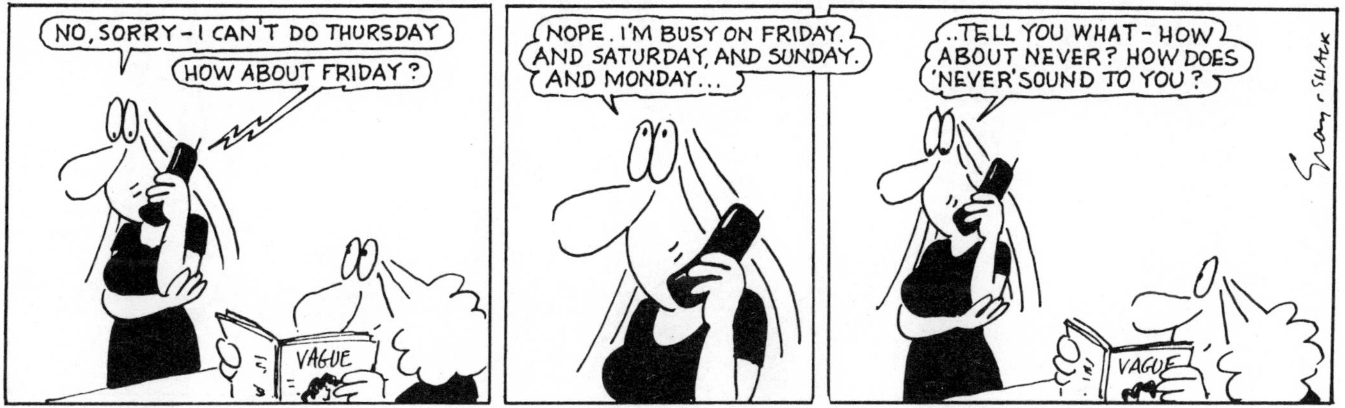
NO, SORRY - I CAN'T DO THURSDAY
HOW ABOUT FRIDAY?
VAGUE
NOPE. I'M BUSY ON FRIDAY. AND SATURDAY, AND SUNDAY. AND MONDAY...
..TELL YOU WHAT - HOW ABOUT NEVER? HOW DOES 'NEVER' SOUND TO YOU?
VAGUE

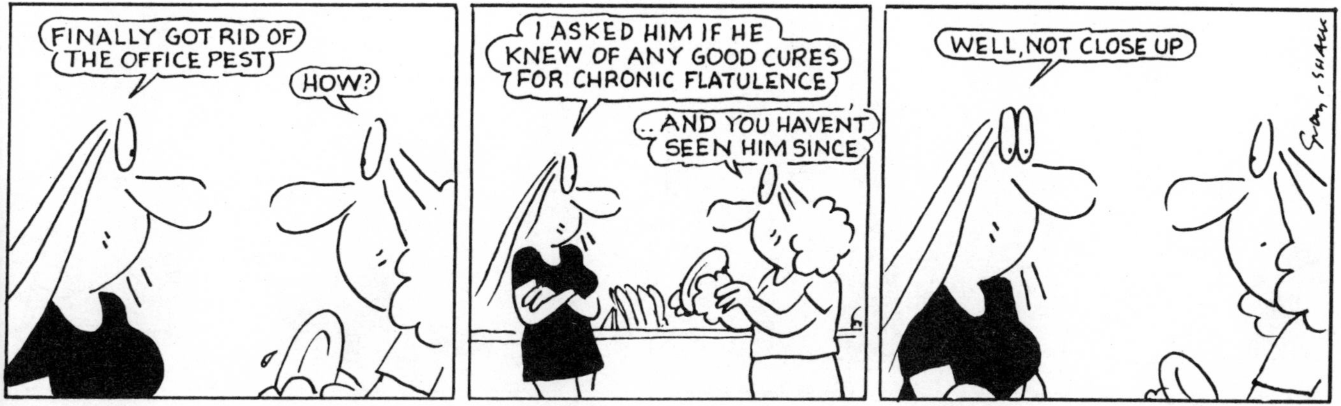
FINALLY GOT RID OF THE OFFICE PEST
HOW?
I ASKED HIM IF HE KNEW OF ANY GOOD CURES FOR CHRONIC FLATULENCE
..AND YOU HAVENT SEEN HIM SINCE
WELL, NOT CLOSE UP

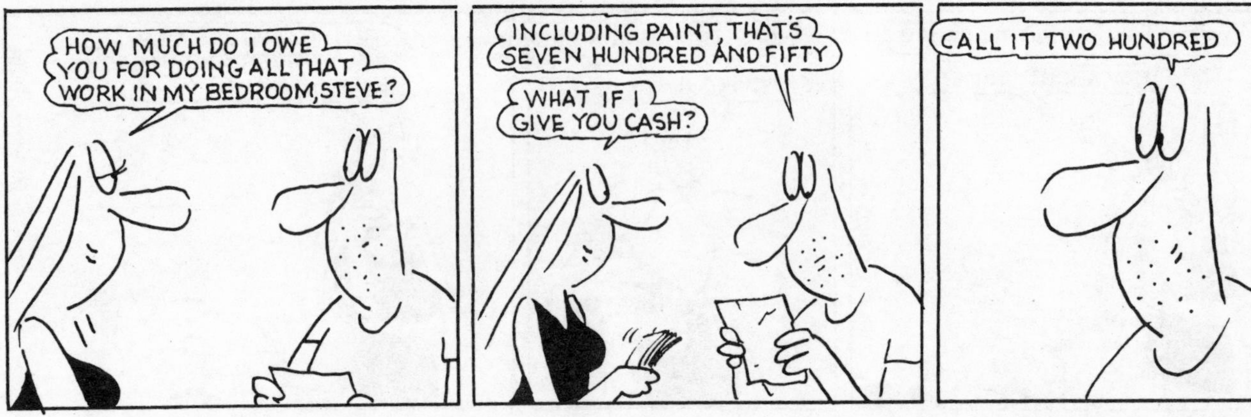
HOW MUCH DO I OWE YOU FOR DOING ALL THAT WORK IN MY BEDROOM, STEVE?
INCLUDING PAINT, THAT'S SEVEN HUNDRED AND FIFTY
WHAT IF I GIVE YOU CASH?
CALL IT TWO HUNDRED

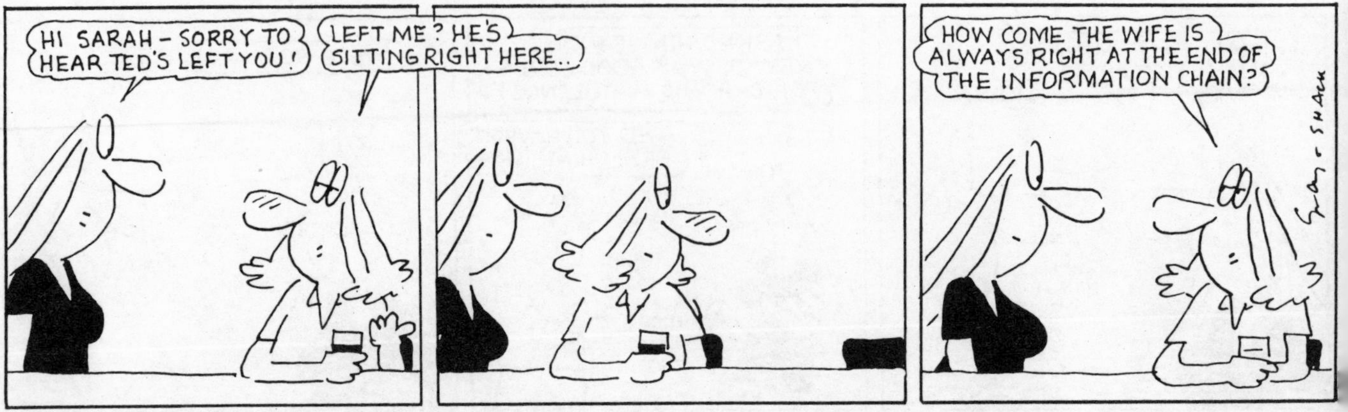
HI SARAH - SORRY TO HEAR TED'S LEFT YOU!
LEFT ME? HE'S SITTING RIGHT HERE..
HOW COME THE WIFE IS ALWAYS RIGHT AT THE END OF THE INFORMATION CHAIN?

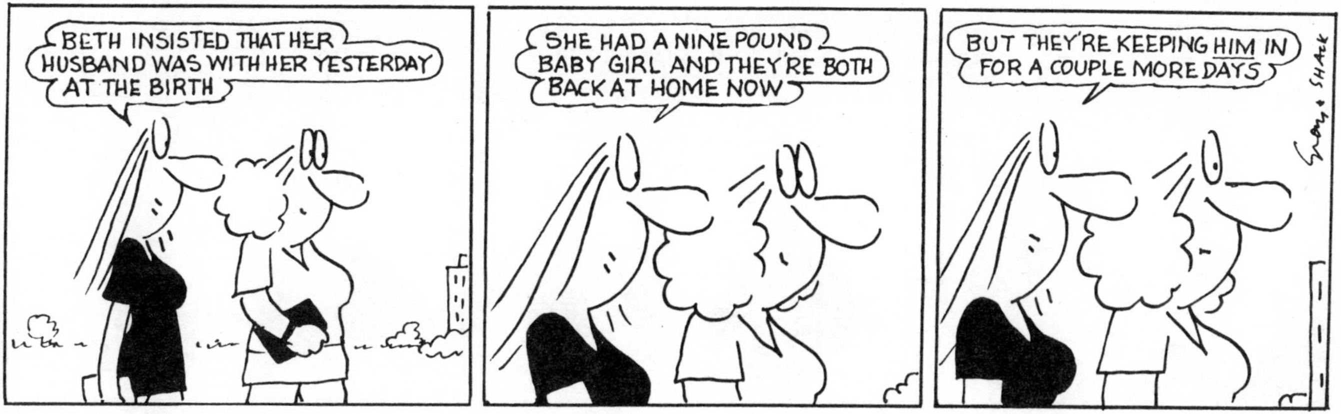
BETH INSISTED THAT HER HUSBAND WAS WITH HER YESTERDAY AT THE BIRTH
SHE HAD A NINE POUND BABY GIRL AND THEY'RE BOTH BACK AT HOME NOW
BUT THEY'RE KEEPING HIM IN FOR A COUPLE MORE DAYS

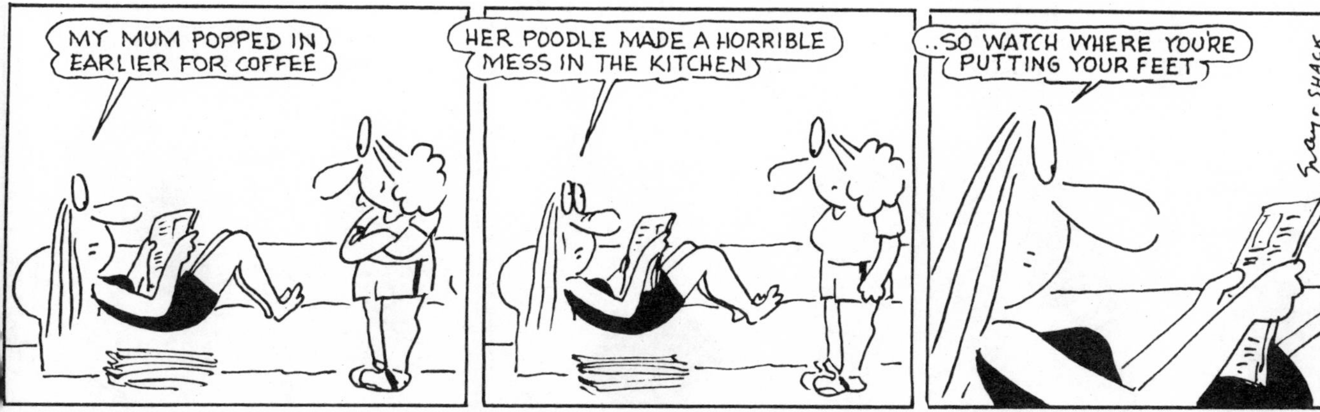
MY MUM POPPED IN EARLIER FOR COFFEE
HER POODLE MADE A HORRIBLE MESS IN THE KITCHEN
..SO WATCH WHERE YOU'RE PUTTING YOUR FEET

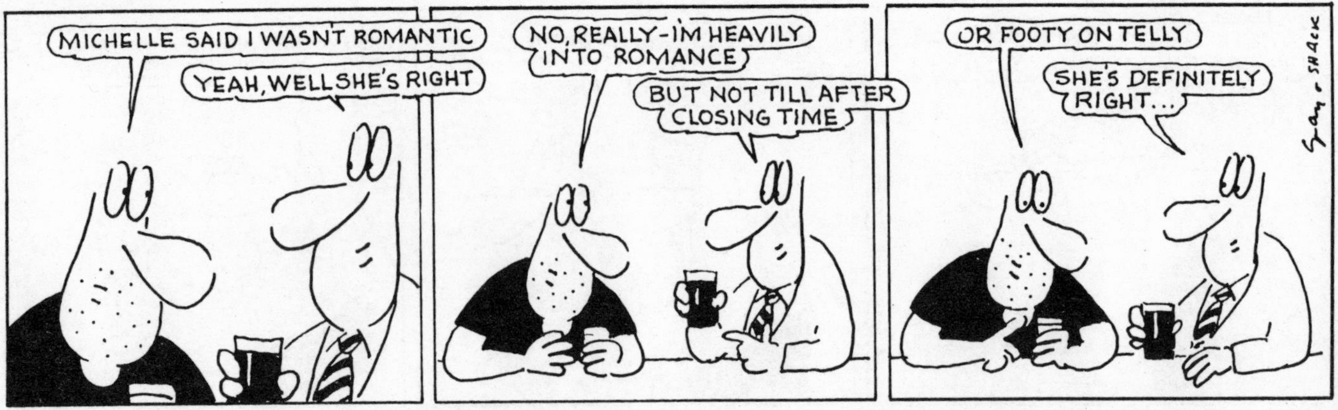
MICHELLE SAID I WASN'T ROMANTIC
YEAH, WELL SHE'S RIGHT
NO, REALLY - I'M HEAVILY INTO ROMANCE
BUT NOT TILL AFTER CLOSING TIME
OR FOOTY ON TELLY
SHE'S DEFINITELY RIGHT...

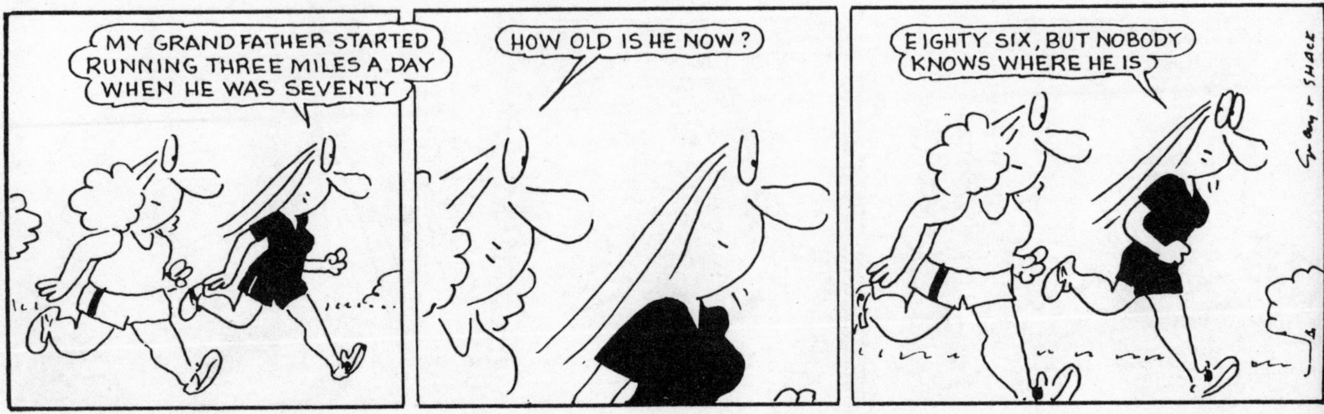
MY GRAND FATHER STARTED RUNNING THREE MILES A DAY WHEN HE WAS SEVENTY
HOW OLD IS HE NOW?
EIGHTY SIX, BUT NOBODY KNOWS WHERE HE IS

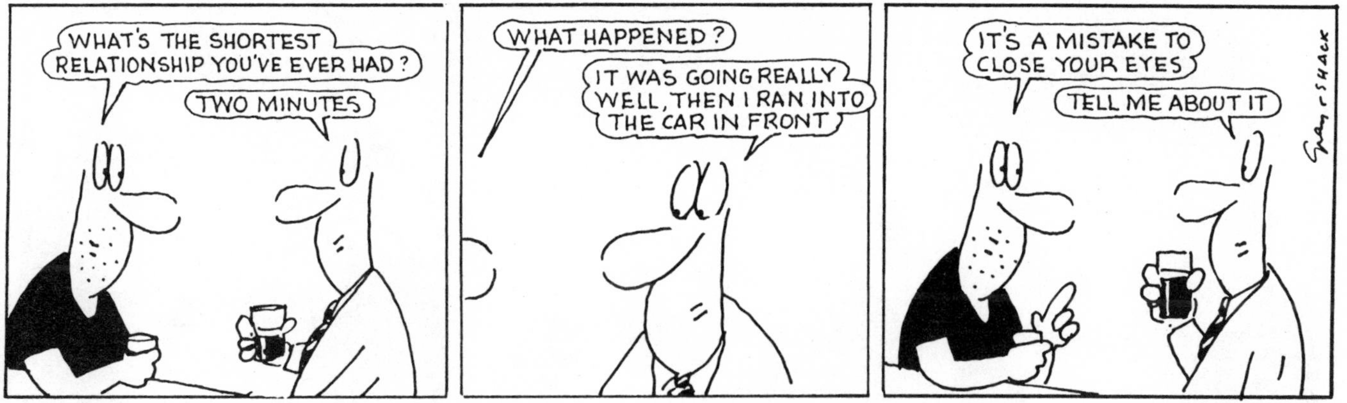
WHAT'S THE SHORTEST RELATIONSHIP YOU'VE EVER HAD?
TWO MINUTES
WHAT HAPPENED?
IT WAS GOING REALLY WELL, THEN I RAN INTO THE CAR IN FRONT
IT'S A MISTAKE TO CLOSE YOUR EYES
TELL ME ABOUT IT

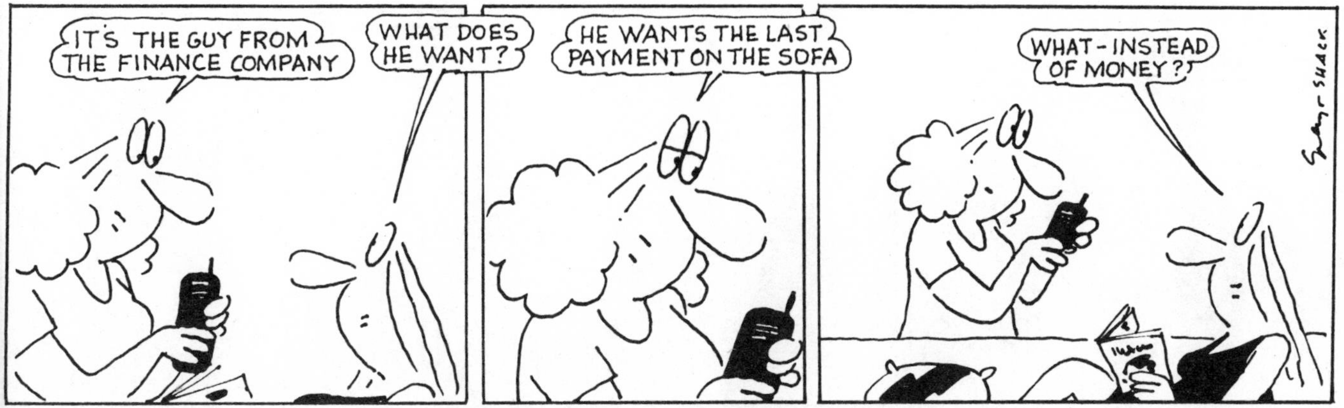
IT'S THE GUY FROM THE FINANCE COMPANY
WHAT DOES HE WANT?
HE WANTS THE LAST PAYMENT ON THE SOFA
WHAT - INSTEAD OF MONEY?

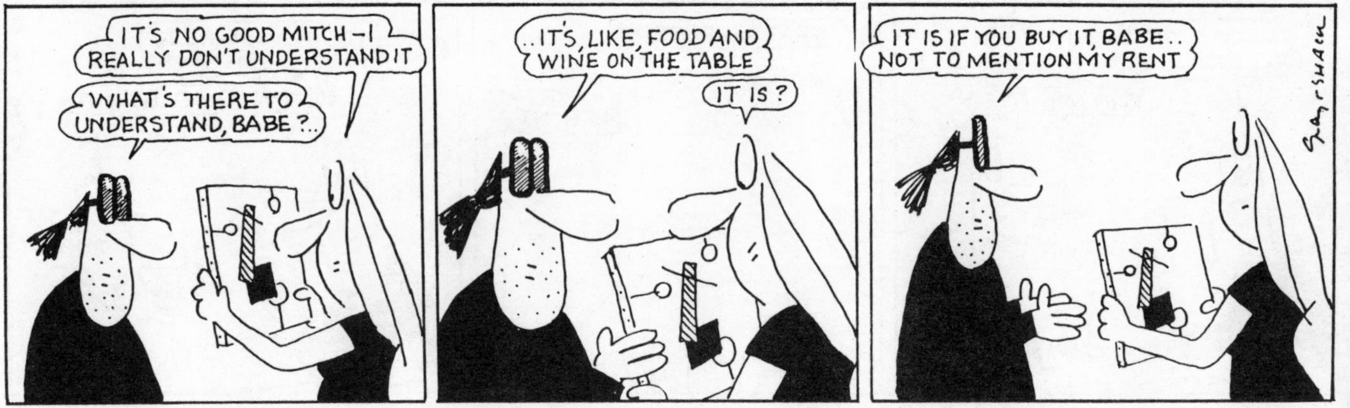
IT'S NO GOOD MITCH – I REALLY DON'T UNDERSTAND IT
WHAT'S THERE TO UNDERSTAND, BABE?..
..IT'S, LIKE, FOOD AND WINE ON THE TABLE
IT IS?
IT IS IF YOU BUY IT, BABE.. NOT TO MENTION MY RENT

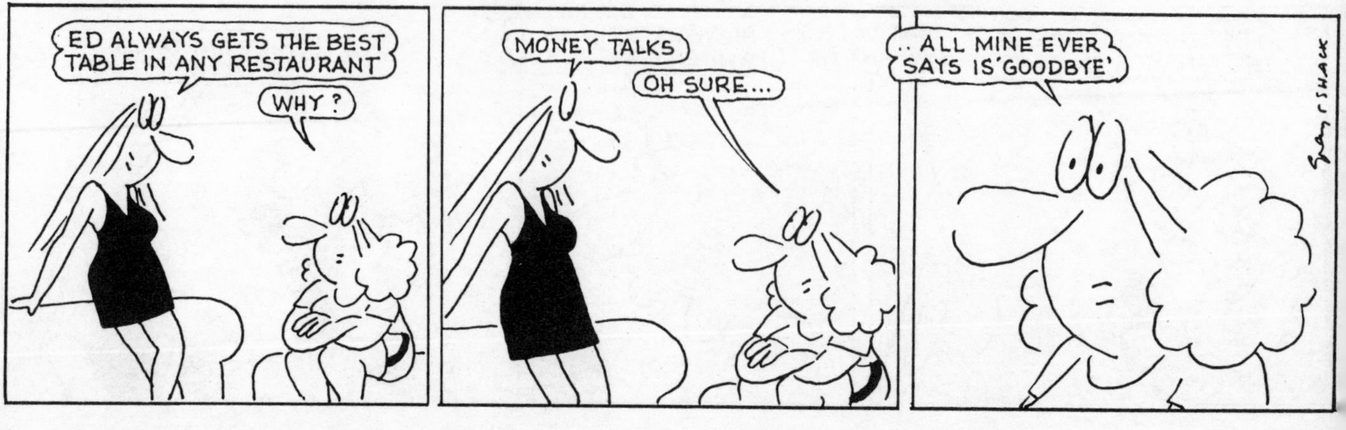
ED ALWAYS GETS THE BEST TABLE IN ANY RESTAURANT
WHY?
MONEY TALKS
OH SURE...
..ALL MINE EVER SAYS IS 'GOODBYE'

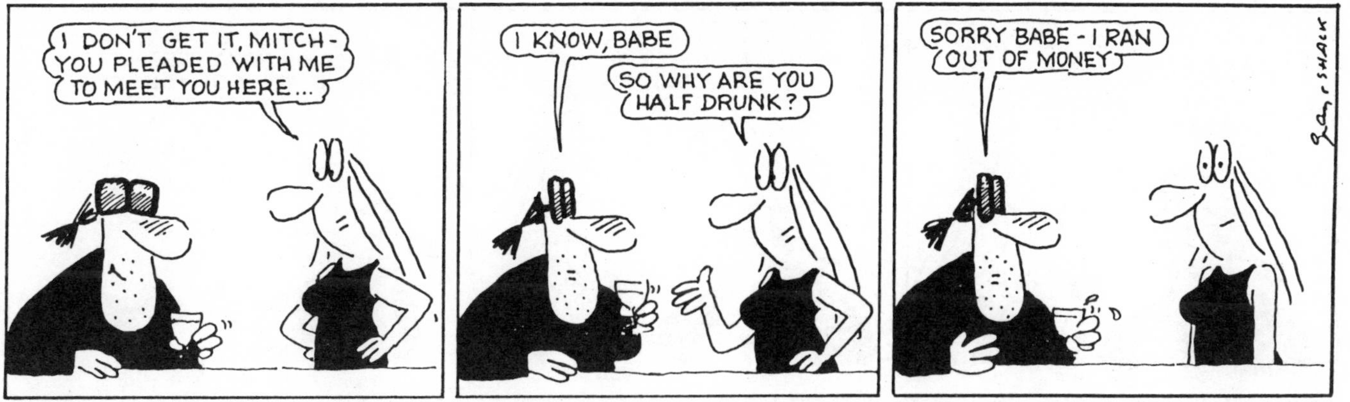
I DON'T GET IT, MITCH - YOU PLEADED WITH ME TO MEET YOU HERE...
I KNOW, BABE
SO WHY ARE YOU HALF DRUNK?
SORRY BABE - I RAN OUT OF MONEY

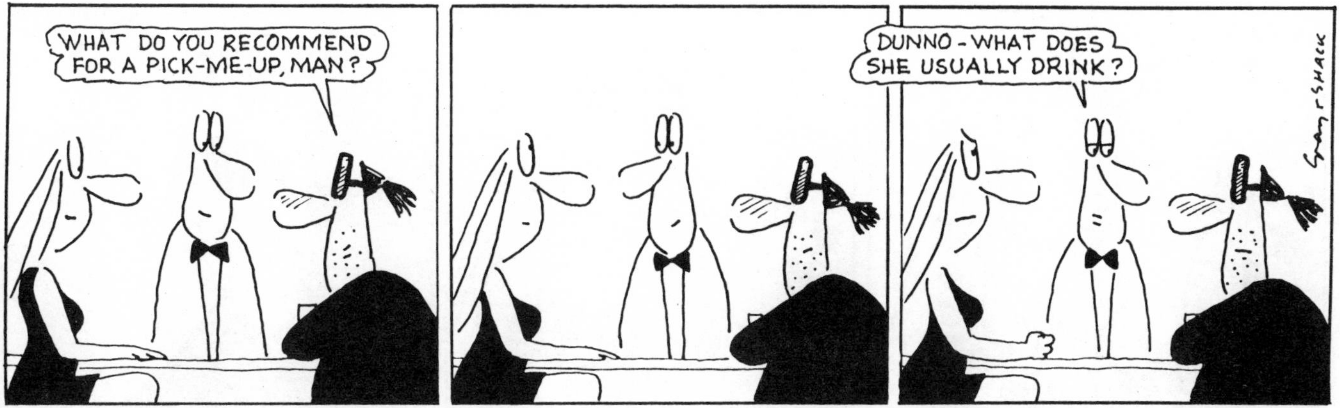
WHAT DO YOU RECOMMEND FOR A PICK-ME-UP, MAN?
DUNNO - WHAT DOES SHE USUALLY DRINK?

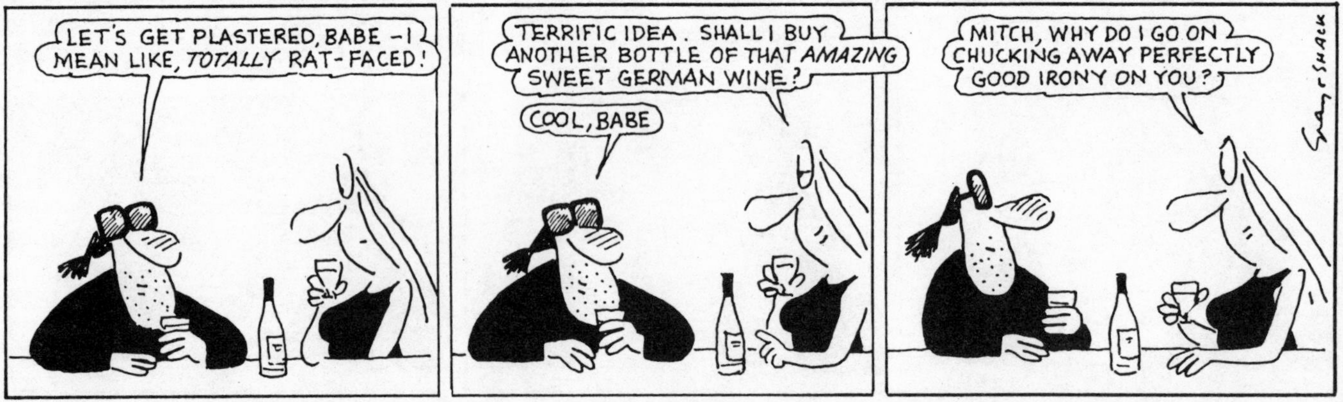
LET'S GET PLASTERED, BABE – I MEAN LIKE, *TOTALLY* RAT-FACED!
TERRIFIC IDEA. SHALL I BUY ANOTHER BOTTLE OF THAT *AMAZING* SWEET GERMAN WINE?
COOL, BABE
MITCH, WHY DO I GO ON CHUCKING AWAY PERFECTLY GOOD IRONY ON YOU?

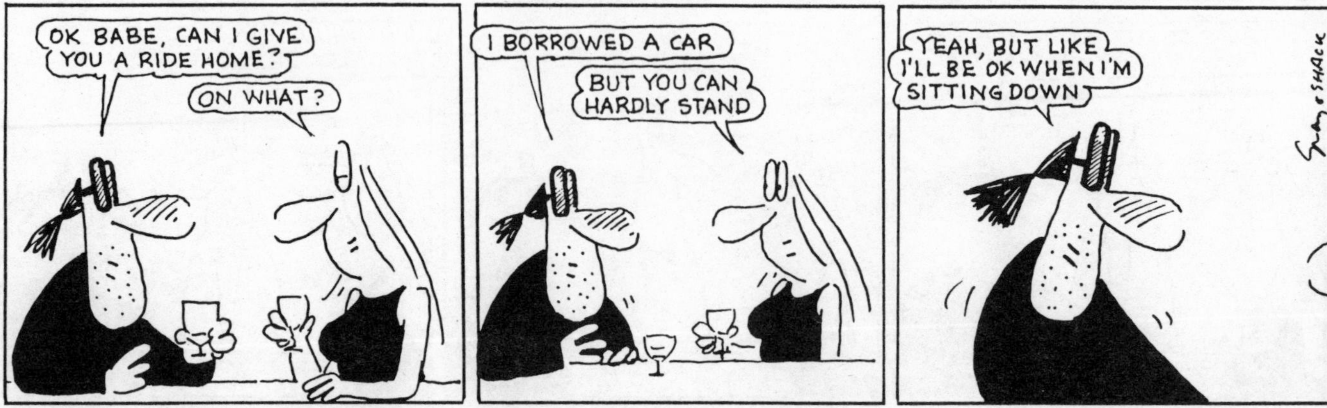
OK BABE, CAN I GIVE YOU A RIDE HOME?
ON WHAT?
I BORROWED A CAR
BUT YOU CAN HARDLY STAND
YEAH, BUT LIKE I'LL BE OK WHEN I'M SITTING DOWN

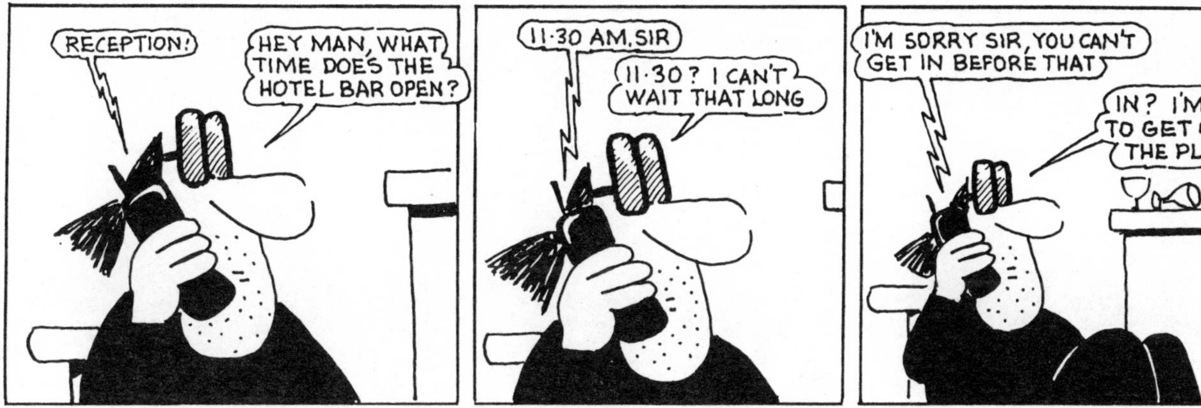
RECEPTION!
HEY MAN, WHAT TIME DOES THE HOTEL BAR OPEN?
11·30 AM, SIR
11·30? I CAN'T WAIT THAT LONG
I'M SORRY SIR, YOU CAN'T GET IN BEFORE THAT
IN? I'M TRYING TO GET OUT OF THE PLACE, MAN

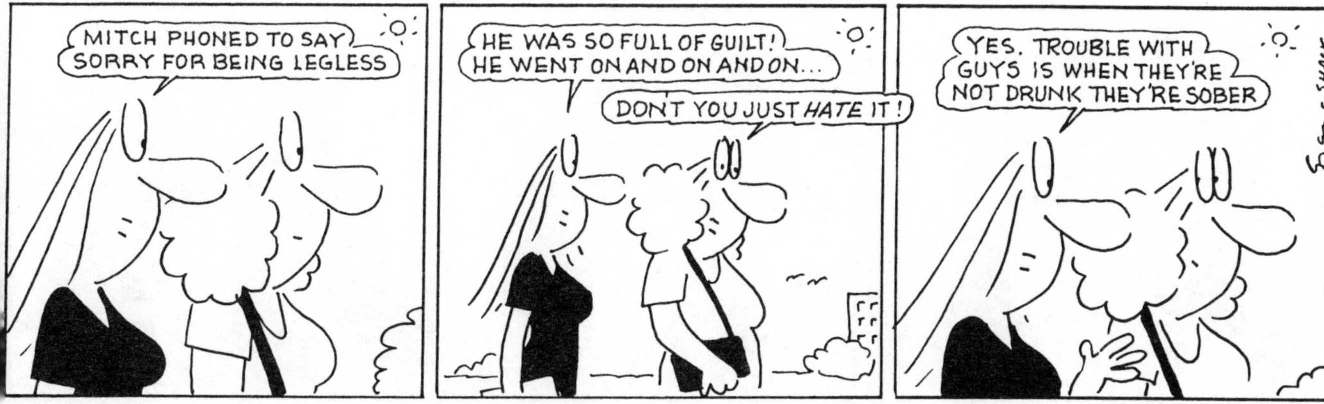
MITCH PHONED TO SAY SORRY FOR BEING LEGLESS
HE WAS SO FULL OF GUILT! HE WENT ON AND ON AND ON...
DON'T YOU JUST HATE IT!
YES. TROUBLE WITH GUYS IS WHEN THEY'RE NOT DRUNK THEY'RE SOBER

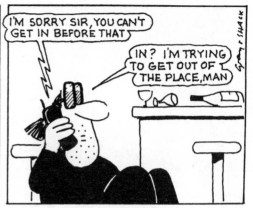

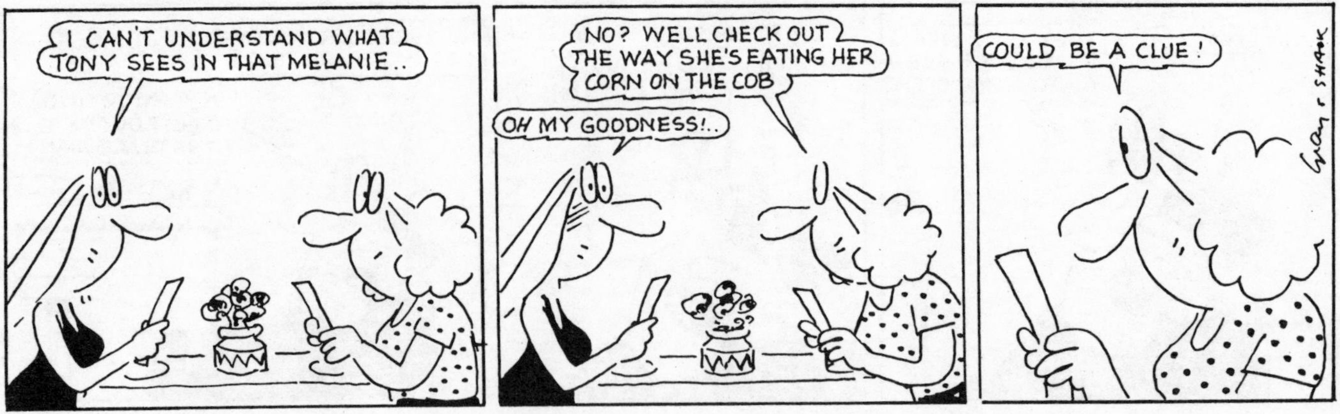
I CAN'T UNDERSTAND WHAT TONY SEES IN THAT MELANIE..
NO? WELL CHECK OUT THE WAY SHE'S EATING HER CORN ON THE COB
OH MY GOODNESS!..
COULD BE A CLUE!

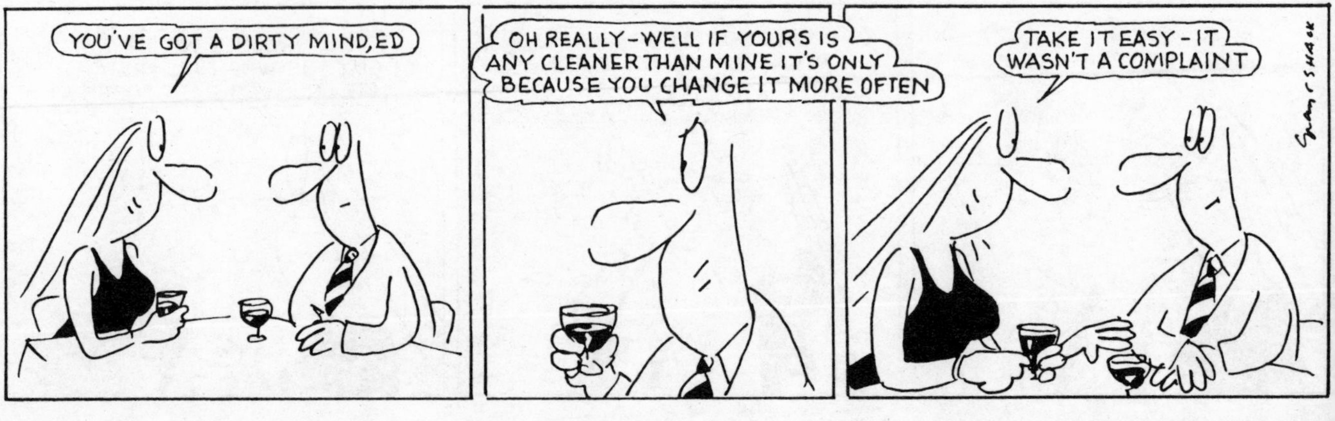
YOU'VE GOT A DIRTY MIND, ED
OH REALLY - WELL IF YOURS IS ANY CLEANER THAN MINE IT'S ONLY BECAUSE YOU CHANGE IT MORE OFTEN
TAKE IT EASY - IT WASN'T A COMPLAINT

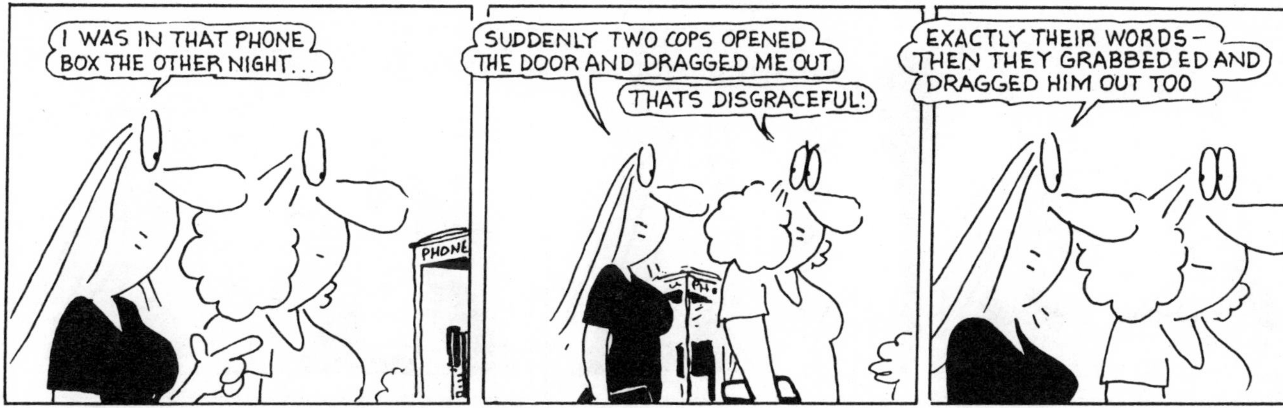
I WAS IN THAT PHONE BOX THE OTHER NIGHT...
PHONE
SUDDENLY TWO COPS OPENED THE DOOR AND DRAGGED ME OUT
THATS DISGRACEFUL!
EXACTLY THEIR WORDS - THEN THEY GRABBED ED AND DRAGGED HIM OUT TOO

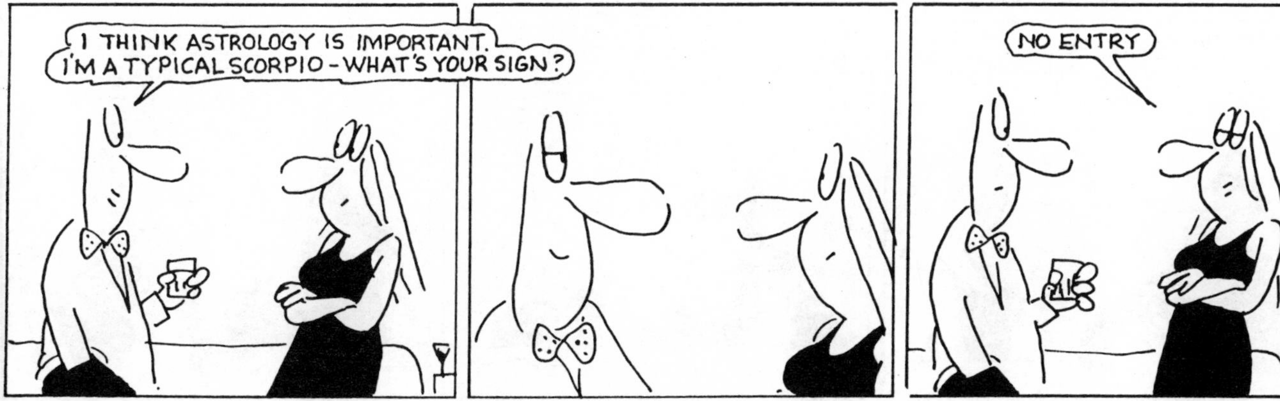
I THINK ASTROLOGY IS IMPORTANT. I'M A TYPICAL SCORPIO - WHAT'S YOUR SIGN?
NO ENTRY

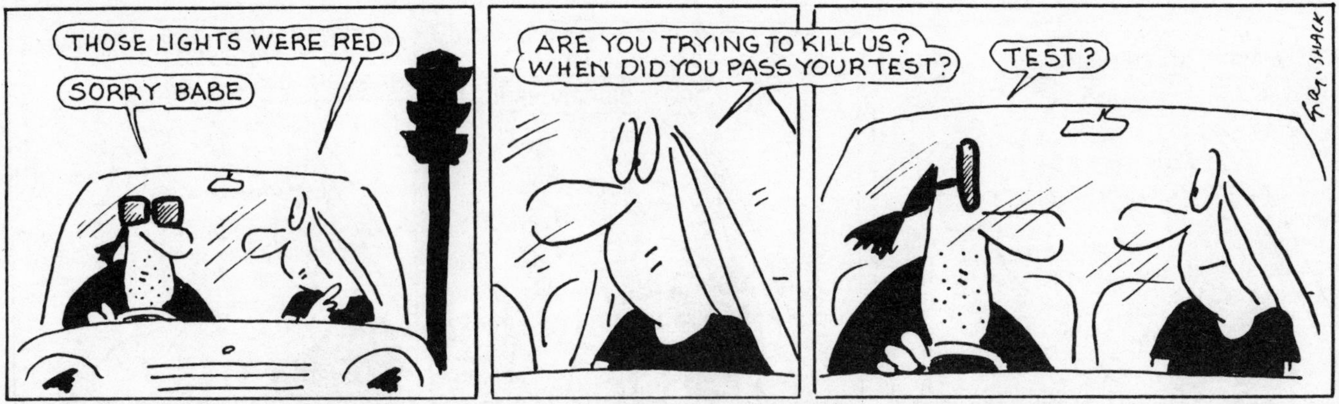
THOSE LIGHTS WERE RED
SORRY BABE
ARE YOU TRYING TO KILL US? WHEN DID YOU PASS YOUR TEST?
TEST?

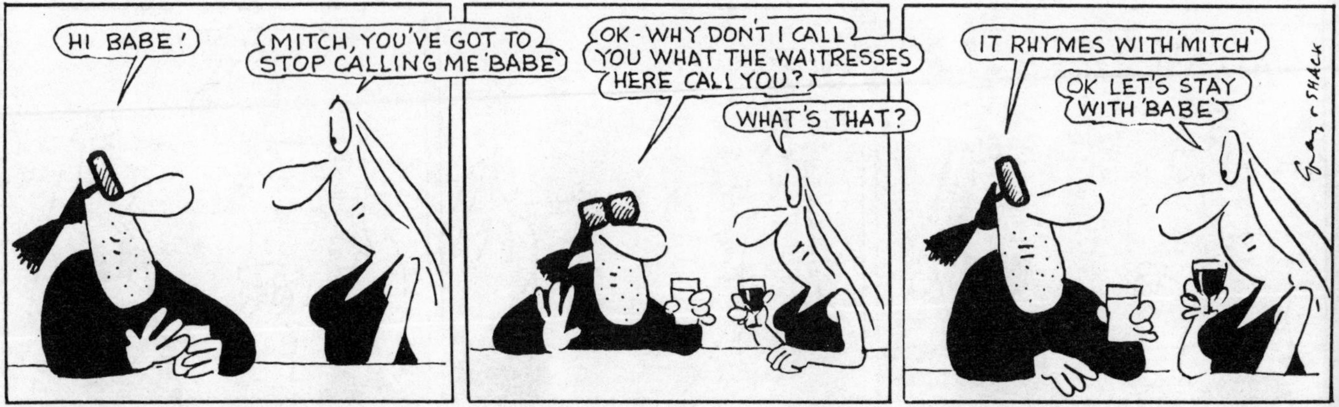
HI BABE!
MITCH, YOU'VE GOT TO STOP CALLING ME 'BABE'
OK - WHY DON'T I CALL YOU WHAT THE WAITRESSES HERE CALL YOU?
WHAT'S THAT?
IT RHYMES WITH 'MITCH'
OK LET'S STAY WITH 'BABE'

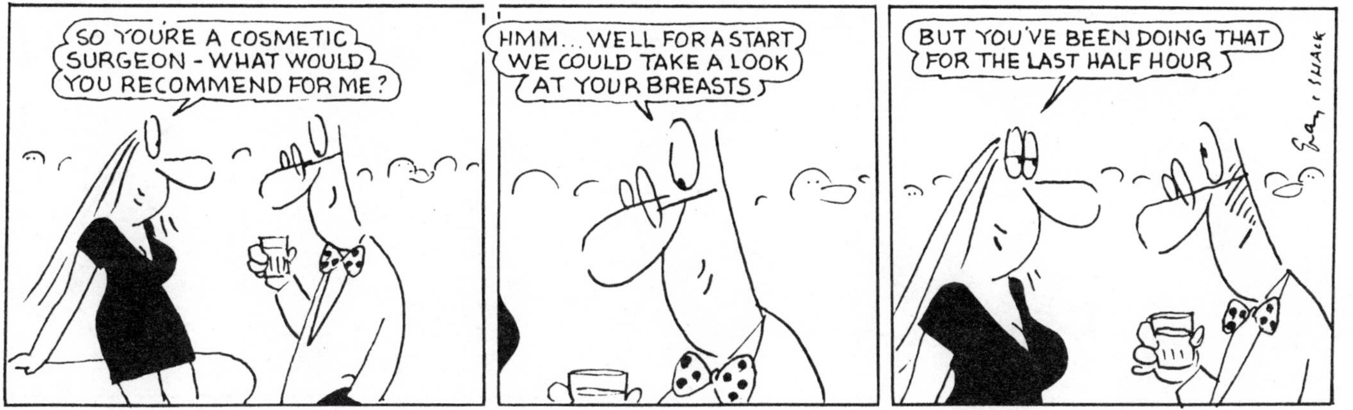
SO YOU'RE A COSMETIC SURGEON - WHAT WOULD YOU RECOMMEND FOR ME?
HMM... WELL FOR A START WE COULD TAKE A LOOK AT YOUR BREASTS
BUT YOU'VE BEEN DOING THAT FOR THE LAST HALF HOUR

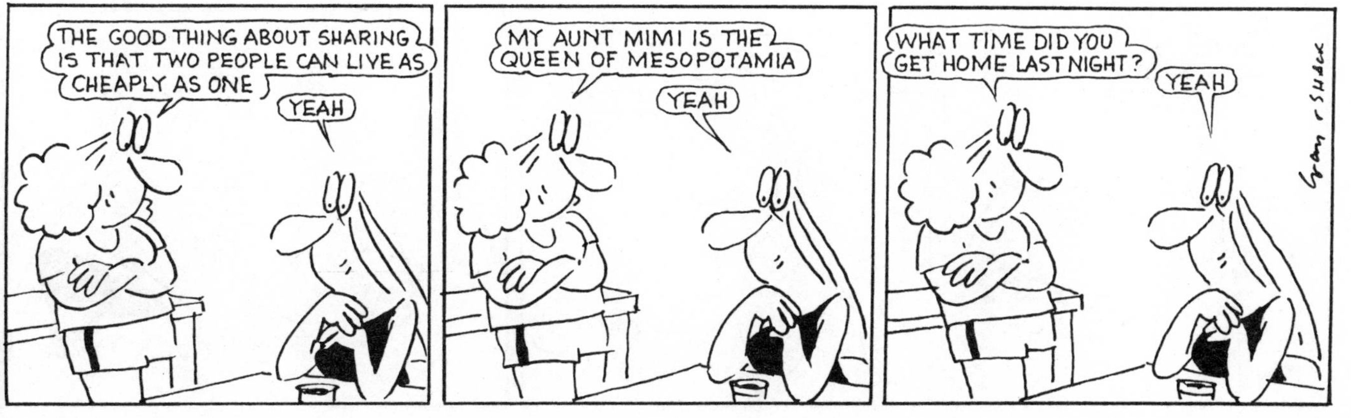
THE GOOD THING ABOUT SHARING IS THAT TWO PEOPLE CAN LIVE AS CHEAPLY AS ONE
YEAH
MY AUNT MIMI IS THE QUEEN OF MESOPOTAMIA
YEAH
WHAT TIME DID YOU GET HOME LAST NIGHT?
YEAH

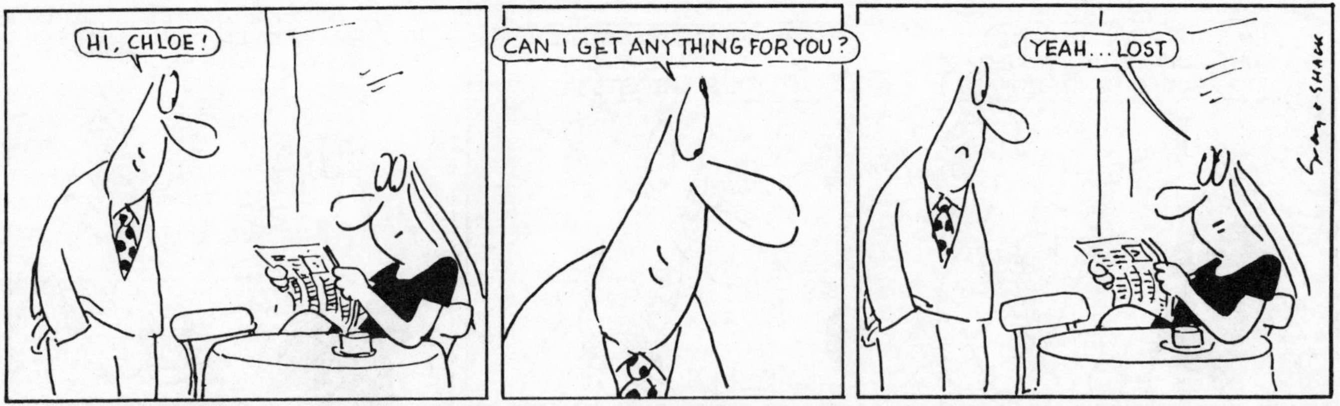
HI, CHLOE!
CAN I GET ANYTHING FOR YOU?
YEAH... LOST

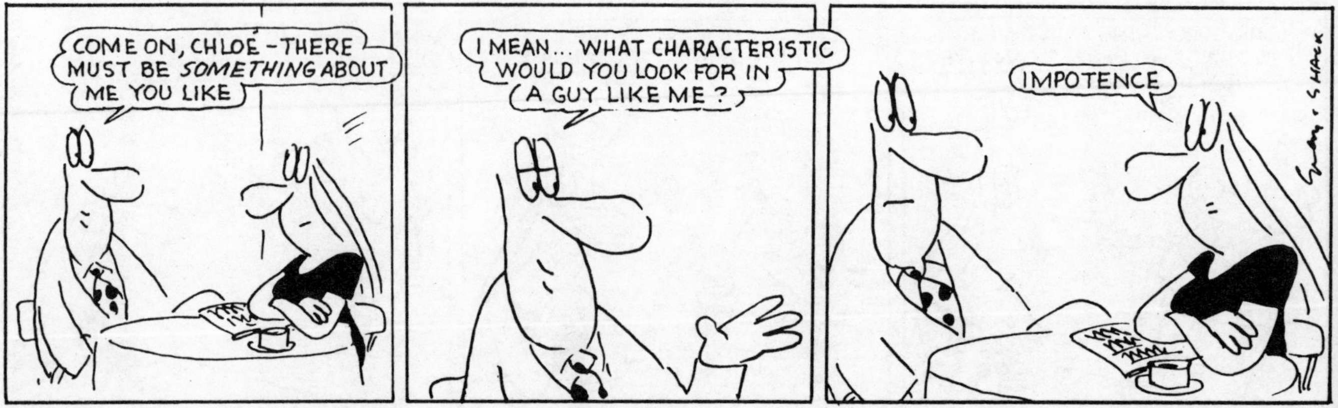
COME ON, CHLOE - THERE MUST BE *SOMETHING* ABOUT ME YOU LIKE
I MEAN... WHAT CHARACTERISTIC WOULD YOU LOOK FOR IN A GUY LIKE ME?
IMPOTENCE

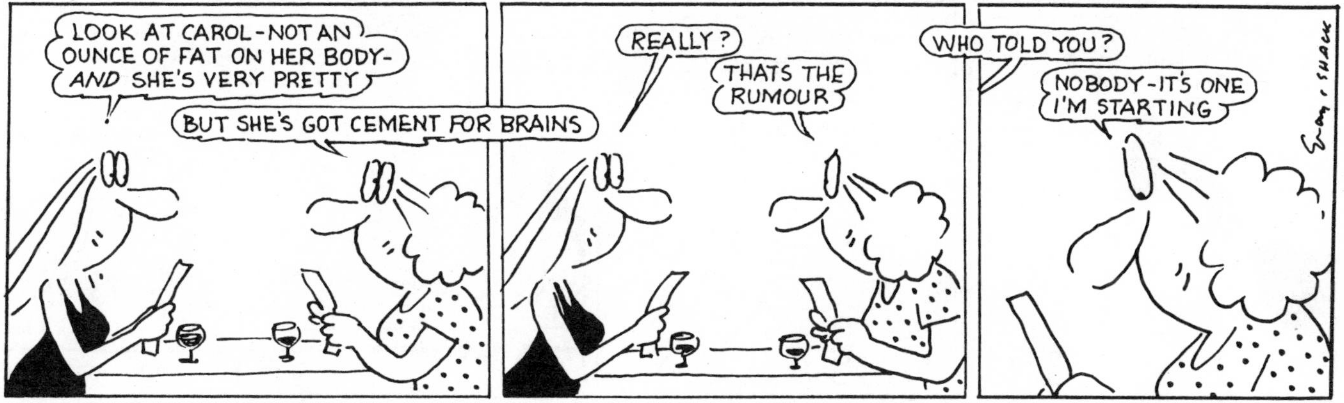

LOOK AT CAROL - NOT AN OUNCE OF FAT ON HER BODY - *AND* SHE'S VERY PRETTY
BUT SHE'S GOT CEMENT FOR BRAINS
REALLY?
THATS THE RUMOUR
WHO TOLD YOU?
NOBODY - IT'S ONE I'M STARTING

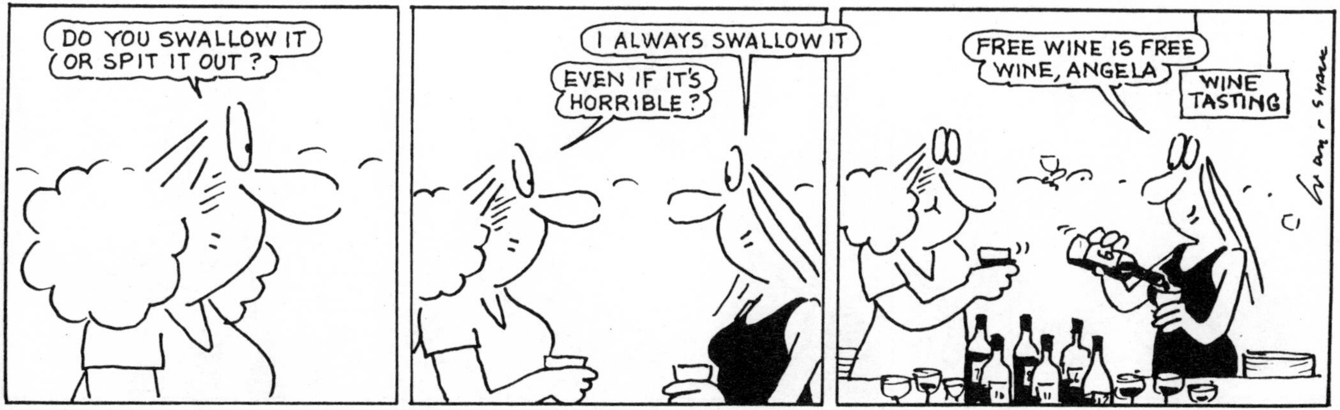

DO YOU SWALLOW IT OR SPIT IT OUT?
I ALWAYS SWALLOW IT
EVEN IF IT'S HORRIBLE?
FREE WINE IS FREE WINE, ANGELA
WINE TASTING

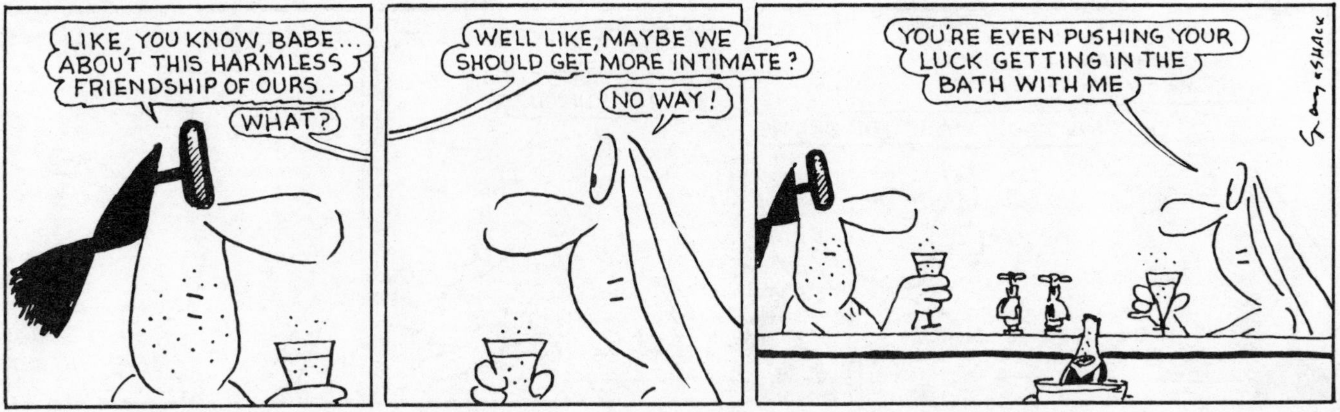
LIKE, YOU KNOW, BABE... ABOUT THIS HARMLESS FRIENDSHIP OF OURS..
WHAT?
WELL LIKE, MAYBE WE SHOULD GET MORE INTIMATE?
NO WAY!
YOU'RE EVEN PUSHING YOUR LUCK GETTING IN THE BATH WITH ME

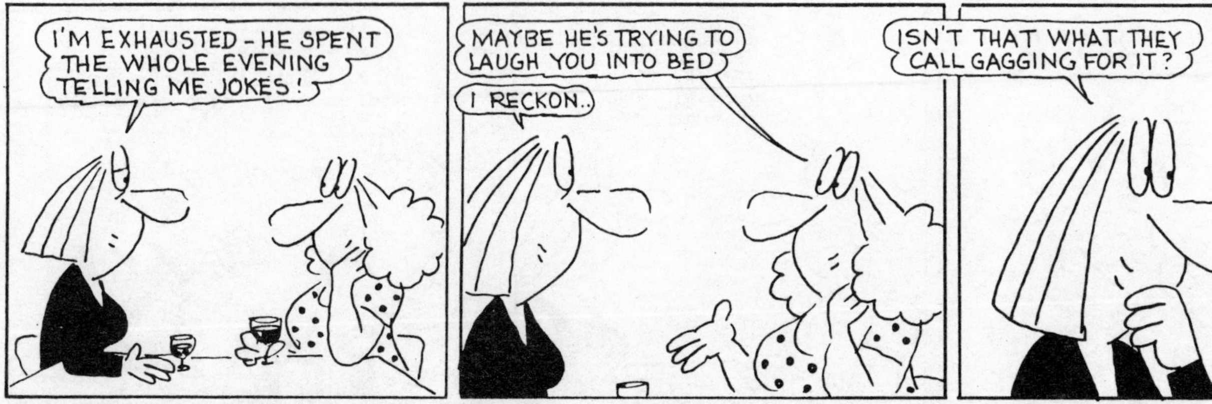
I'M EXHAUSTED - HE SPENT THE WHOLE EVENING TELLING ME JOKES!
MAYBE HE'S TRYING TO LAUGH YOU INTO BED
I RECKON..
ISN'T THAT WHAT THEY CALL GAGGING FOR IT?

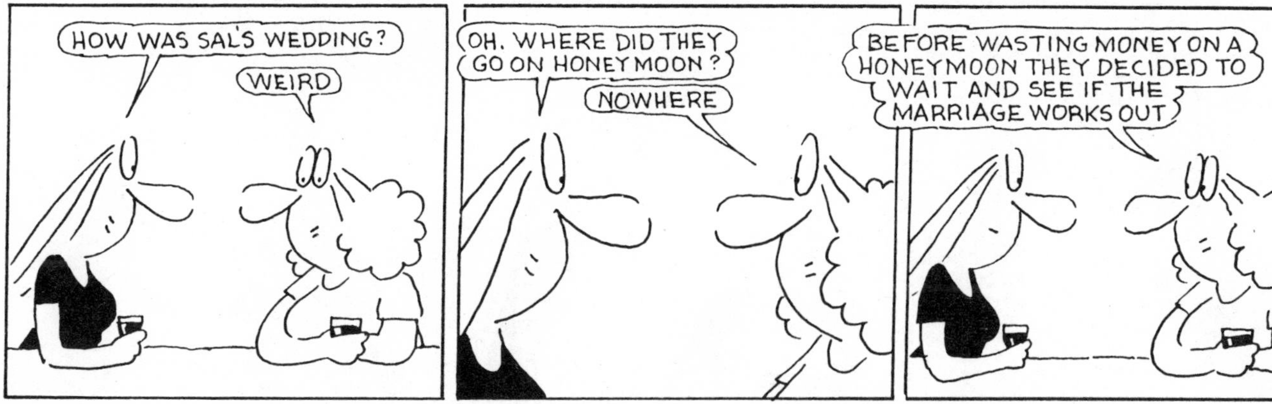
HOW WAS SAL'S WEDDING?
WEIRD
OH. WHERE DID THEY GO ON HONEYMOON?
NOWHERE
BEFORE WASTING MONEY ON A HONEYMOON THEY DECIDED TO WAIT AND SEE IF THE MARRIAGE WORKS OUT

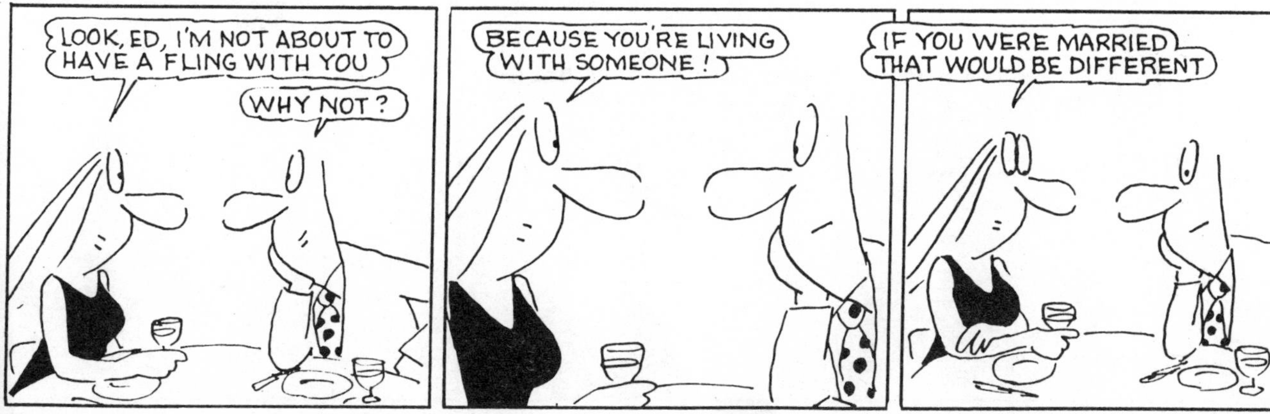
LOOK, ED, I'M NOT ABOUT TO HAVE A FLING WITH YOU
WHY NOT?
BECAUSE YOU'RE LIVING WITH SOMEONE!
IF YOU WERE MARRIED THAT WOULD BE DIFFERENT

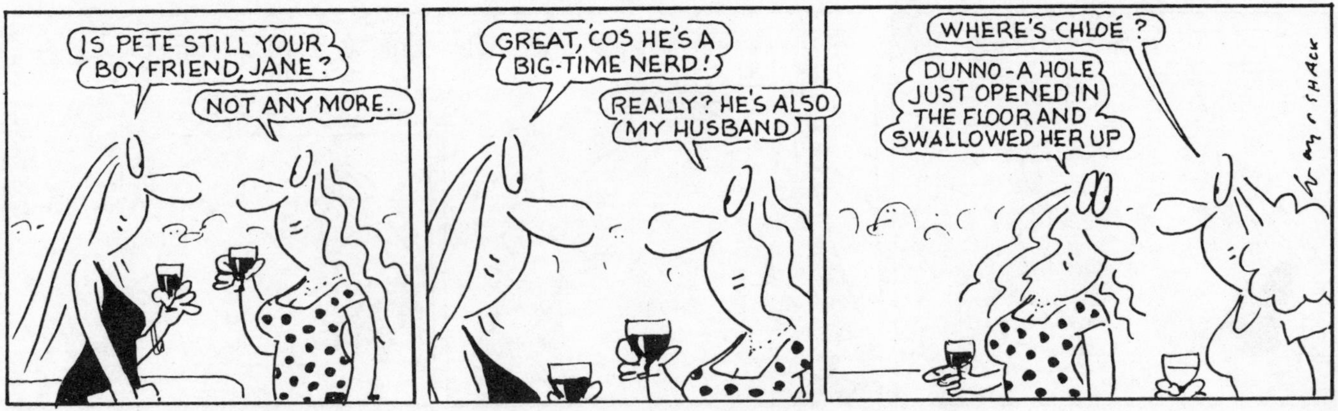
IS PETE STILL YOUR BOYFRIEND, JANE?
NOT ANY MORE..
GREAT, COS HE'S A BIG-TIME NERD!
REALLY? HE'S ALSO MY HUSBAND
WHERE'S CHLOÉ ?
DUNNO - A HOLE JUST OPENED IN THE FLOOR AND SWALLOWED HER UP

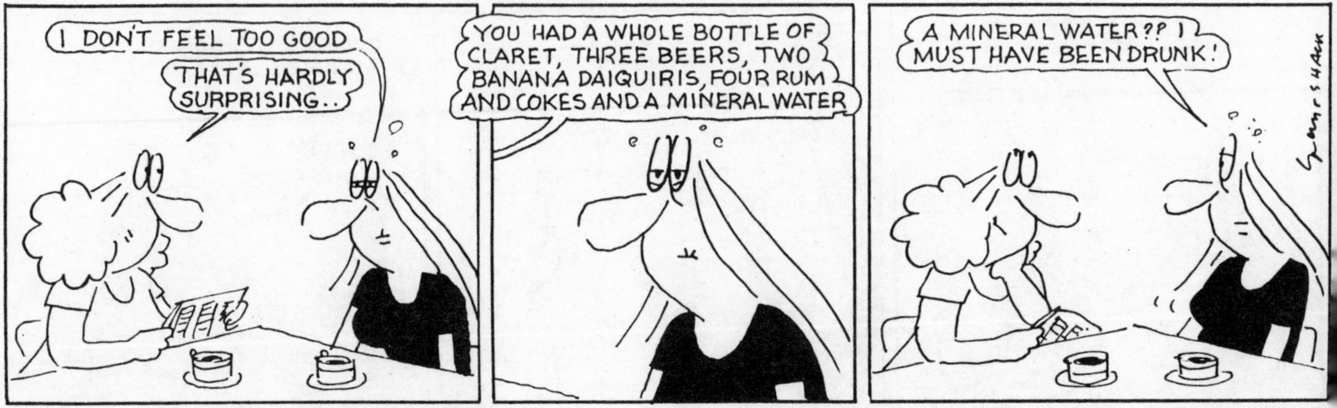
I DON'T FEEL TOO GOOD
THAT'S HARDLY SURPRISING..
YOU HAD A WHOLE BOTTLE OF CLARET, THREE BEERS, TWO BANANA DAIQUIRIS, FOUR RUM AND COKES AND A MINERAL WATER
A MINERAL WATER?? I MUST HAVE BEEN DRUNK!

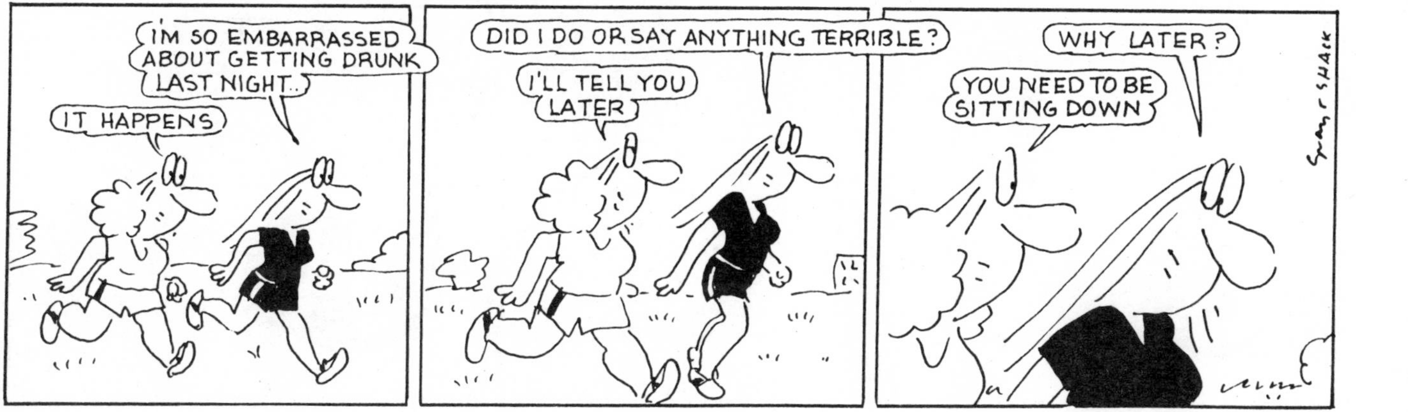
I'M SO EMBARRASSED ABOUT GETTING DRUNK LAST NIGHT..
IT HAPPENS
DID I DO OR SAY ANYTHING TERRIBLE?
I'LL TELL YOU LATER
WHY LATER?
YOU NEED TO BE SITTING DOWN

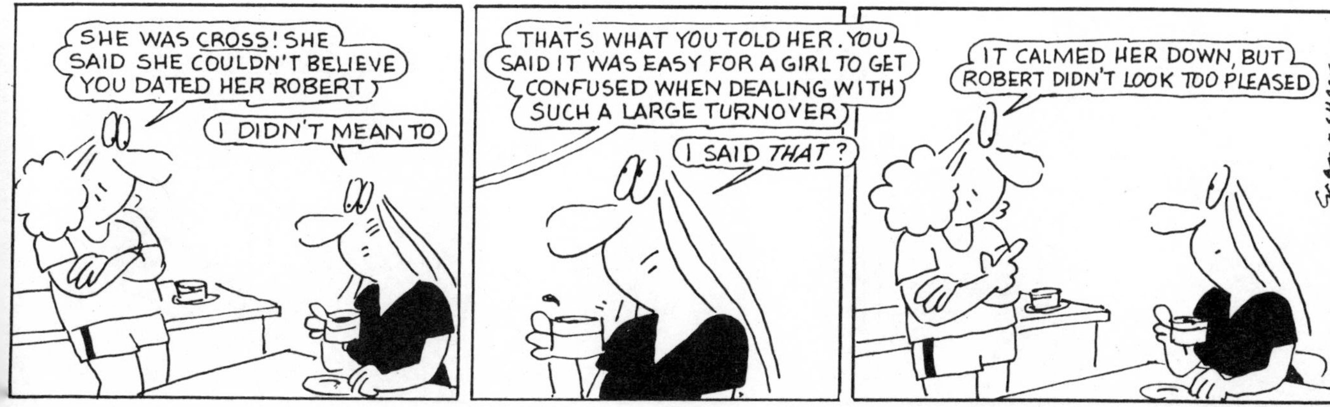
SHE WAS CROSS! SHE SAID SHE COULDN'T BELIEVE YOU DATED HER ROBERT
I DIDN'T MEAN TO
THAT'S WHAT YOU TOLD HER. YOU SAID IT WAS EASY FOR A GIRL TO GET CONFUSED WHEN DEALING WITH SUCH A LARGE TURNOVER
I SAID *THAT*?
IT CALMED HER DOWN, BUT ROBERT DIDN'T LOOK TOO PLEASED

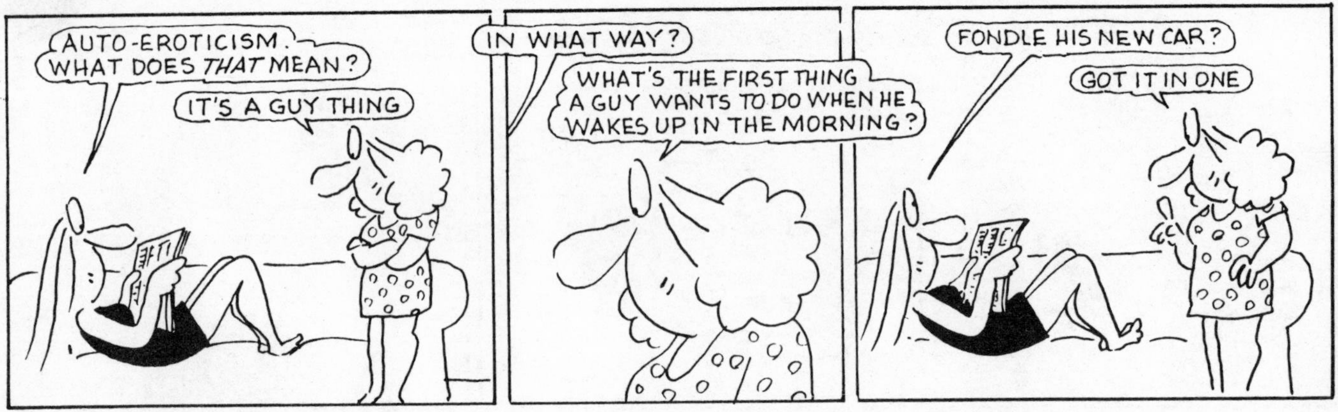
AUTO-EROTICISM. WHAT DOES *THAT* MEAN?
IT'S A GUY THING
IN WHAT WAY?
WHAT'S THE FIRST THING A GUY WANTS TO DO WHEN HE WAKES UP IN THE MORNING?
FONDLE HIS NEW CAR?
GOT IT IN ONE

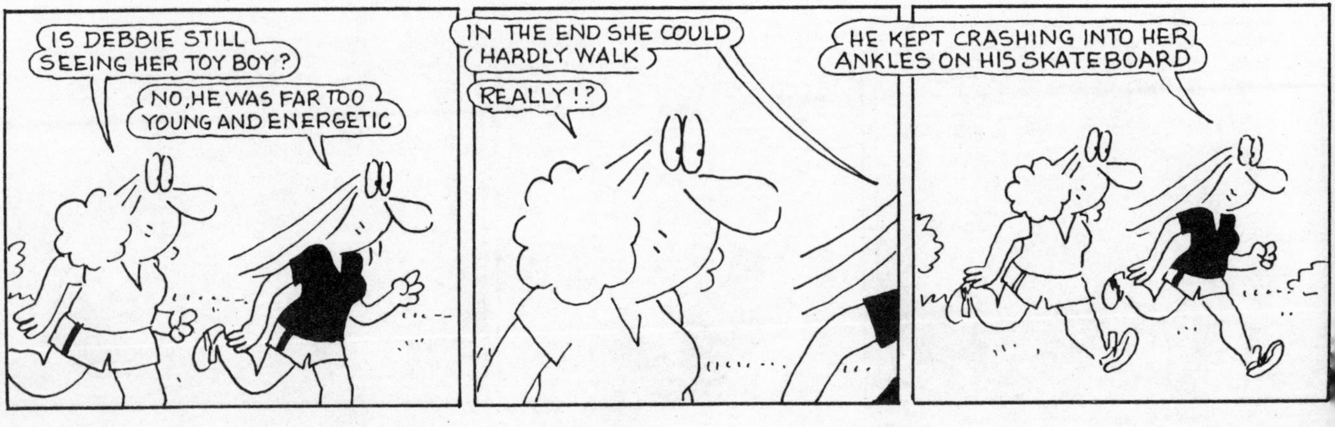
IS DEBBIE STILL SEEING HER TOY BOY?
NO, HE WAS FAR TOO YOUNG AND ENERGETIC
IN THE END SHE COULD HARDLY WALK
REALLY!?
HE KEPT CRASHING INTO HER ANKLES ON HIS SKATEBOARD